Other Books by Thelma T. Reyna

ॐ

FICTION:

The Heavens Weep for Us and Other Stories (2009)

POETRY:

Breath & Bone (2011)
Hearts in Common (2013)
Rising, Falling, All of Us (2014)
Reading Tea Leaves After Trump (2018)
Dearest Papa: A Memoir in Poems (2020)

AS EDITOR:

Altadena Poetry Review: Anthology 2015
Altadena Poetry Review: Anthology 2016

When the Virus Came Calling

Calling

COVID-19 Strikes America

Thelma T. Reyna
Editor

Golden
Foothills
PRESS

Published by Golden Foothills Press
Pasadena, CA 91104
www.GoldenFoothillsPress.com
goldenfoothillspress@yahoo.com

Grateful acknowledgment is made to editors and publishers for permission to reprint poems previously published elsewhere. Credit for prior publication is provided in footnotes at the end of each previously published work.

ISBN 978-0-9969632-7-5

Cover photo: "Sad woman looks nostalgically at her lover's empty chair," #760944613, www.shutterstock.com; slightly modified for this book.
Author photo, back cover: Victor Cass
Cover design: Victor Cass and Dom Gilormini
Book design: Thelma T. Reyna
Interior photo credits: Photos in *Authors' Gallery* provided by authors or accessed in online media with authors' approval.

Printed in the United States of America

First Edition: 2020

Advance Praise:
When the Virus Came Calling

This anthology asks and answers the question: What do the poets of America make of all this? With heartbreaking truths and vivid, precise language, a diverse group of poets and prose writers explore the ruin COVID has made of our lives....Debuting when we are still not able to say where we are in this journey, these revealing meditations offer an uncensored vision of what has happened and serves as a historical/cultural artifact of these times as we plunge forward into the unknown.

—Carla Rachel Sameth
Author, *One Day on the Gold Line: A Memoir in Essays*

Thelma Reyna has assembled a time capsule, a scrapbook, a poetic testimony for those who will undoubtedly peer back from the future to see and experience, on a level beneath the surface, what the COVID-19 pandemic did to a conscious species, globally, in a few months' time. The excellent writers in this book share fears, attitudes, emotional burdens, in a visual, compelling way....a way to transcend, and perhaps survive, the pestilence....so we will remember the jagged road on this early part of our journey.

--Jack G. Bowman
Award-Winning Poet
Author of *Eucalyptus Rex* and *Metamorphic Consequences*

A work of art that captures experiences and reflections of selected award-winning poets from throughout the U.S. This important work commemorates first-person observations and imaginations in diverse ways.... Readers gain new insight through the poets' eyes.

--Kathee Bautista, Ph.D.
Professor, Azusa Pacific University

A truly significant collection of poetry and prose...an anthology of "poetry of witness" of the COVID-19 with diverse voices and viewpoints that surprise us with their takes on this societal and life-altering apocalyptic epidemic. They reflect our families, the workers, and those impoverished on the fringes as these writers share their accounts of isolation, loss, and struggle to survive.

--Vibiana Aparicio-Chamberlin
International Latino Book Awards Winner
Author/Illustrator of *Mi Amor, A Memoir*

A cross-section of social and cultural diversity, the authors here open the windows of their hearts and souls to help us understand the impact of the coronavirus...on them, their friends, and their families. This anthology chronicles their thoughts and feelings, ...their cautions, and fears for future generations. Books such as this will serve as a valuable literary resource for historians.

--Mira N. Mataric, Ph.D.
National, International Award-Winning Poet
Translator, & Educator

Poets observe and their words help us process difficult and seemingly inexpressible experiences.... This powerful poetry anthology begins to pave the healing path out of collective trauma, isolation, and loss.

-- Jennifer Dotson
National Award-Wnning Poet
Author of *Late Night Talk Show Fantasy & Other Poems*
Founder of www.HighlandParkPoetry.org

This anthology is a poignant reminder of our humanity in this time of chaos and fear, reminding us of who we are as a people, and as a global community. The poems resonate with feeling, compassion, empathy, and being a part of the human experience, celebrating the light and darkness of the human spirit. These wonderful authors have come together to paint a safe space for us to grieve what was and what has been lost. Knowing life will never come back again like it was, this book also gives hope for a better and brighter tomorrow.

--Monteque Pope-Le Beau
Publisher & Founder, *The Art Of Monteque*
International Poet & Artist
www.theartofmonteque.com/

When the Virus Came Calling

COVID-19 Strikes America

Thelma T. Reyna

Editor

For the 169,000+ lives lost in the United States.
For the 5.3+ million souls infected and wondering
if they or their loved ones will be alright.
For the healthcare workers
who fight and who have died for the stricken.
For the frontline workers in all endeavors
who risk their lives to keep our nation functioning.
For the California farmworkers who finally
got tested as a vulnerable essential group in August.
*For the governors who **fight the fight** when federal leaders don't.*
For survivors determined to rebuild a better nation for all humanity.

[NOTE: Numbers above as of August 14, 2020]

Foreword
From the Editor

*"Art is not always about pretty things. It's about who
we are, what happened to us, and how our lives are affected."*
--Steele Thomas Marcoux

So it is with this anthology: it has lyrical, "pretty" writings that gladden and lift spirits in our present time of tragedy, but it largely examines our devastating pandemic and how it has deeply changed our lives. The gravitas, reflectiveness, and insights of the authors here indeed elucidate "who we are, what happened to us, and how our lives are affected."

Although the COVID-19 outbreak has ravaged the globe, this book focuses only on the American experience with it. It details the progression of this novel coronavirus in our homeland, from its arrival in January 2020, through the final months of summer, describing how it swiftly changed our routines, our work, family lives, careers, relationships, economy, and politics *in real time*, in the words and emotions of poets and prose writers who open their hearts and lives to us.

And what a cast of "historians" this is, gifting us, the readers, their news and revelations, providing us different artistic lenses through which to view the turbulence of this year. What we have in this book are "primary sources" of information elucidating a historic event, for COVID is a once-in-a-100-years epidemic of cataclysmic scope. Their writings are divided into four sections arranged chronologically through these pivotal first months of the crisis.

The authors represented here were hand-picked from across the nation and personally invited to write poetry or prose, as they chose, while our nation and their lives were changing daily. Rising to the task with their deep experience and skills, our writers collectively are:

- Present or past Poets Laureate
- National and/or regional literary award-winners
- Nominees for the famed Pushcart Prize in Poetry
- Published authors of at least one book
- Editors and/or publishers of literary journals, blogs, anthologies, or individual books
- Poetry community leaders: curators of literary events, workshop leaders, and public reading event coordinators
- Professors and/or instructors of writing at different institutions throughout America
- Writers in multiple genres: poetry, fiction, and nonfiction.

Just as important, our authors represent the beautiful tapestry of American diversity: ethnic, cultural, geographic, socioeconomic, generational, and political. Some are immigrants or the children of immigrants. Some are emerging writers, blossoming in their art. Others are mentors in the prime of their evolution. The breadth and depth of their diversity lend their words even greater humanity and representativeness. We are grateful to them.

Also, just as important: As this book neared its final stages of pre-production, George Floyd was killed on the street in Minneapolis on May 25 by a police officer, catapulting America into months of daily protest marches traversing our nation and countries around the globe. Millions of protestors marched into the night, young and old people of all ethnicities, to demand justice and build a better nation.

In the midst of our historic pandemic, these protestors risked their health and lives to speak out. Inevitably, these cataclysmic events intertwined: tales of sudden suffering, swift death, danger, risk, hope, resilience, devotion…and love. This book thus includes some poems and personal essays about the convergence of these monumental events.

--Thelma T. Reyna
Pasadena, CA
August 2020

Introduction

by Robin D. G. Kelley, Ph.D.

Distinguished Professor and Gary B. Nash Endowed Chair in U.S. History, UCLA

Writer, critic, revolutionary Arundhati Roy famously described a pandemic as "a portal, a gateway between one world and the next."[1] Poetry is also a portal, a gateway through the imagination between the world as it was, as it is, and as we wish it to be. It is also a portal through which the heart's ineffable feelings of pain, joy, grief, rage, confusion, and exultation are transformed into words. Poetry allows us to imagine a different future, helps us decide what we want to carry forward and what we ought to leave behind. Poetry binds us together even as it celebrates our difference. And poetry is the most potent weapon we have in the fight to build our world anew.

Thelma Reyna understands this better than any poet I have ever encountered. Knowing that poets are truly first responders, she has boldly chosen to confront the worst global pandemic in modern history by gathering some of the country's finest poets and prose writers to reflect on the tragic and empowering dimensions of crises, and to create a portal to "another world." This book is a *collective* response to a world overwhelmingly marked by suffering and death. A world where illness and loss touches each and every one of us. A world where confinement and social distance are the conditions to think about freedom. A world where healthcare workers, most of whom are black and brown immigrants or children of immigrants, risk their lives under a government willing to boost spending on police, the military, and border walls while spending almost nothing

13

on the personal protective equipment our frontline and medical heroes desperately need.

When COVID-19 struck, most Americans were already facing a litany of crises. The pandemic exacerbated bad situations, at times serving as a pretext for indifferent politicians to ramp up unconscionable policies. Laws protecting workers were ignored, as retail and warehouse workers, gig workers, transit and municipal workers, laborers in the meatpacking industry and farm fields fought for their lives as infection rates rose exponentially. Indian country became a coronavirus epicenter in the U.S., thanks largely to the federal government's continued legacy of neglect. Prisoners and prison staff became the most vulnerable, with 80% of the inmates at Ohio's Marion Correctional Institution, and over one-third of San Quentin's population, testing positive for COVID-19.

We saw a spike in anti-Asian racism provoked by the myth that "Chinese" are carriers. Cases of domestic violence spiked, as many women have been forced to choose between homelessness and "sheltering in place" with abusive partners. Meanwhile, *armed* White militias showed up at public rallies and on the steps of state capitols, defying their state's legal social distancing measures and demanding an immediate end to "stay at home" orders. After years of watching footage of unarmed Black people beaten and killed by police for walking, loitering, running, standing in front of their homes, showing insufficient deference, protecting their kids, being a kid, these scenes of angry White men storming their state legislature while it was in session, brandishing AR-15s in the face of police and government officials, and evading jail, injury or death, begs incredulity.

And then, on May 25, as some states began to open up, the world watched a video of Minneapolis police officer Derek Chauvin pressing his knee into the neck of a handcuffed, unarmed black man named George Floyd, Jr. who, pinned to the asphalt, repeatedly begged for his life. We heard Floyd summon his dead mother minutes before joining her. Millions of people grabbed their masks and took to the streets, risking exposure to COVID-19 to face down riot police, tear gas, rubber bullets, all to demand justice for Floyd and an end to state-sanctioned racial violence. The protesters had much to lose but a new world to gain.

Great poetry looks catastrophe in the eye, stares it down, and penetrates its terrifying exterior to find its core, its seed, its soul. Poetry can find beauty in ugliness and collect knowledge from unlikely places. And so it is with the poets in this anthology, who listen to the voices of the suffering, the fearful, and the unheard—children, animals (roosters, turkeys, dogs, rabbits, squirrels, *los pájaros saben*), and "Mother Earth." They remind us that we're living through a man-made disaster, begun centuries ago when certain men sought to create wealth in other lands, turn human beings into beasts of burden, build factories and pipelines, and strip the soil of nutrients polluting our water, creating inequality, and suppressing knowledge people have carried to make us safe and healthy. This is where plagues and pestilence come from, and this is why all of our sophisticated knowledge can't stop it.

The great poet Aimé Césaire taught us in 1945, that, "Poetic knowledge is born in the great silence of scientific knowledge."[2] Césaire's point was that we need poetic knowledge to understand and move us beyond the world's crises. Even when this crisis passes and

the next is upon us, we need this book. We need to read these poems —
every single one — and the prose pieces in this book, and carry them
with us everywhere we go. The portal they have opened takes us not to
a "new normal" but a new world — a world that rejects the
normalization of violence, exploitation, dispossession, racism, sexism,
xenophobia, and greed.

Once again, Arundhati Roy summons us: "We can choose to
walk through [a pandemic], dragging the carcasses of our prejudice and
hatred, our avarice, our data banks and dead ideas, our dead rivers and
smoky skies behind us. Or we can walk through lightly, with little
luggage, ready to imagine another world. And ready to fight for it."[3]
This book shows us this as well.

---

[1] Arundhati Roy, "The Pandemic is a Portal," *Financial Times* (April 3, 2020),
https://www.ft.com/content/10d8f5e8-74eb-11ea-95fe-fcd274e920ca

[2] Aimé Césaire, "Poesie et Connaissance," Tropique 12 (January 1945), translated
and reprinted as "Poetry and Knowledge" in *Refusal of the Shadow: Surrealism and
the Caribbean*, trans. by Michael Richardson and Krzysztof Fijalkowski (London:
Verso, 1996), 134-145.

[3] Arundhati Roy, "The Pandemic Is a Portal."

Contents

i.
. . . invasion
{January/February}

ii.
. . . seclusion
{March}

iii.
. . . introspection
{April / May}

iv.
. . . realizations
{June / July}

෨

i.
. . . invasion

{January/February}

First case in the U.S.:   January 20, 2020
First death in the U.S.:   February 29, 2020
[retroactively identified]

Bloom

Today ideas bloom
want poetry to make
a difference in a world

gripped by fear and not knowing
how can poets make a difference
how can they help us breathe

how can they give us moments
filled with words that cause us
to laugh think feel be

let each of us as poets create
words that feed our souls
free our minds make us thankful
to be alive

what can we do to till the soil
what can we do to calm the wind
let each of us as poets create
hope to relish sun on our face

rain on our backs and trees flowers
animals who "shine for us"
show off their best by just being there

We are the words
We are the readers
We are the ones who walk in the rain
between raindrops

We are the ones who light up the dark
keep door of possibilities ajar
We are the ones who offer our
poems as a gift to the world

One word at a time.

--Gerda Govine Ituarte

Facts and Fearlessness

My millenial friend
told me he believed
this was just a political diversion
and also, a damn good time
to buy plane tickets
to far away places.

My wise woman friend
hair streaked by the ashes of years past
told me not to drink
their Corona Kool-aid
and still goes out to shop
for her own groceries.

I linger in the space between
their 50 years of difference,
somewhere between 26 and 76.
A full spectrum exists, it seems,
between their disbelief.
In the middle of this spectrum I reside. I order
groceries online and I don't
have any plans to travel.

Instead, I have a mask.

And I have plans. Plans
to try and incorporate, when this
is over, some of their fearlessness
into my world. I, too, was fearless
at 26. And I believe I will be fearless
at 76, when my hair is streaked

by the ashes of years past. But I would
like to see those years, so my fearlessness
is tinged with reservation
trepidation
doubt
and the facts. Facts and fearlessness
can be bedfellows. In the middle of the two,
I don my mask
for a morning walk.

--Amy L. Alley

This year's Corona COVID-19

Here we go. Again.
Corona's annual shade.
It's time we blanked out.

I went through this twice.
Fifty-seven Sixty-eight.
A million dead each.

Something's changed. Techno.
Intrusion fades. Welcome screens.
Fears become cravings.

How quickly distance
Becomes the new social norm.
Jacked into our screens.

When it fades away
Our phones will own us more than
We've ever been owned.

Tracked. Measured. Owned. Gone.
Who will you be in this space?
With all walls torn down.

Plug in. Turn off. Dream.
Devil's nightmares, blissful smiles.
Corona? Who cares?

--Michael Haussler

At the Start of the Pandemic, We Find Ourselves in the Desert

The moon opened over my bed like a dangerous blossom,
a corolla, a whorl unfurled, a silver pistil pointed this way.
In the desert, everything is aiming for your life.

I have come here to sleep among the Joshua trees
where a small bird lands in between the pricked
leaves—a flare of iridescent green and violet—

spread like an infection across the neck. It's hard to stop
moving when your heart beats 500 times a minute.
It's hard to stop feeling like you're running out of time.

Here on Serrano land, after the Spanish, after smallpox,
it's all bayonets and spines. The news has us on edge.
WHO declared the outbreak a pandemic today,

named it *corona*, spikes orbiting the virus like a crown.
How a cactus wren builds a nest inside a teddy bear
cholla. How we hope to take shelter in a world of thorns.

--**Linda Dove & Angie Vorhies**

Crows

Sun rise shiny black crows
line up on telephone wire
observe us new homeowners

Squawk their discontent
eyes track our movements
perhaps they want to reclaim what was

Is this an omen of what's to come
once before when a dear friend died
crows showed up flapped wings furiously

Across horizon circled around and around
blue sky faded grey clouds gathered
My body trembled

This time of urgency crows swarmed northwest
high-pitched cries exploded deafened
red tail hawk circled ready for a fight

To catch newborns in their nests
crows morphed into kamikaze pilots on patrol
Hawk razor sharp eyes hooked beak claws

Could not break through lines of defense
headed west a black dot in the blue
crows turned east some settled in their nests

Three birds glide on security watch
silhouettes against an orange sky
as sun dips below mountains

A universal reality protect our children keep
predators at bay forage for food never-ending
cycle of survival

--Gerda Govine Ituarte

Mother Earth Speaks

I gave you boundless fields
golden in autumn sun.
You poisoned them.

I gave you noble beasts
to roam the veldt.
You slaughtered them to hang their heads on office walls.

I gave you hills of verdant hues and
forests unending.
You clear-cut them.

I gave you oceans
rich with reefs and fish.
You tossed your waste into the sea.

I gave you windswept deserts;
you sucked oil from their bellies
to fuel your greed.

I gave you birds and butterflies
to delight your souls.
You were too gluttonous to see.

I gave you air, fresh as falling snow.
Fumes from your factories, ash from your smokestacks
blackened skies, choked children.

It has come to this:

I give you back
the waters you defiled.
Floods and polluted rivers are now yours.

I give you drought and starvation
and mighty winds, fires unceasing
to bend your will.

I give you back
all you have given me:
Plague and pestilence abound.

It has come to this.

--Judie Rae

COVID-19 as a Disney Movie

The movie opens on a typical, sunny day. There are fluffy clouds in the blue sky and a breeze is gently toying with the trees. A river splashes merrily and small cute animals abound.

Tinkerbell is flitting around winking coyly in her green bustier and sprinkling pixie dust randomly into the air. Pluto thinks this is so much fun. He runs around with his mouth open to catch the magic dust. Pluto inhales wrong and he coughs and sputters.

Sneezy happens to be passing by and inhales some fairy dust and Pluto's cough. Sneezy goes home and sneezes on the other dwarves who then sneeze on Snow White. Snow White then sneezes at Prince Florian turns his head but is so captivated by Snow White's beauty that he just *has* to kiss her.

The Fairy Godmother, passing through after a visit to Cinderella stops to see Snow White and Prince Florian. Prince Florian, ever the gentleman, kisses her hand when she arrives. The Fairy Godmother tears up at the act of kindness and wipes her eye with her hand.

Her next stop is a visit to Belle and The Beast and when she arrives she uses her magic wand to help Belle clean up. Sparkles from the wand land on surfaces and The Beast and everyone in the castle are glittery.

A week later, Belle and The Beast start to feel ill. When Beast puts two and two together he flies into a rage and runs out into the forest.

Shere Khan happens to be passing by and Beast starts to roar at him but instead vomits all over his tigery body. Shere Khan runs to the nearest river to wash off, while just downstream, John Smith fills his canteen on his way to meet his beloved, Pocahontas.

TO BE CONTINUED...

--Khadija Anderson

Windowsill Prayer: A Precursor to COVID-19

for Stacey

Let me polish my grief
like stones from the creek
    lucky stones
pulled from time's passage
and brought home
to stay on the sill
quite well-oiled,
        still.

Let me feel the refrain
of repetition each day
in prayers and thoughts
that otherwise
       like birds
would fly away.

Let me feed them, my soul,
it's hard to survive,
to let yourself feel
and still be alive –
to shake the quilt of open spaces
of open spaces
that so few can have
while COVID-19 cuts
its wide swath.

Let my sadness shine in tears,
      warm and salty.
      compassionate,
        real.

                --Carolyn Clark

Foreshadowing

yesterday
I woke to
streets absent crows' caw
no car horns no screeching brakes
workers' drills gone from the building next door
today
low melodic medleys of swallow and wren
why am I
grateful for almost silence

neighborhood park
baby turtles climb from the pond
fall back in
a duck family promenades across the grass
yesterday four young ones
today three

Pacific Palisades
ocean view through chain link fence
yesterday a woman skated by
threw her mask to the curb
today a man strides down the street shouts
in June there will be 20,000 dead
we will all die we will all die

yesterday
bumblebees in the plum blossoms
today
trees suddenly green
where will we be when
first fruit falls

--Nancy Shiffrin

Day Six

Books shake on the shelves

      Water is sipped like a fine cognac

Eat slow and chew longer

      Notice the art on the wall and details on family photos

Talk to planets

      Watch the cat on catnip trip

Watch doomsday flicks

      Get rejections in the mail

Nothing is the same, yet nothing has changed

      I still miss the flowering of the night-blooming cereus

Dogs continue their barking

      I still enjoy my coffee before the city wakes

A few incarcerated souls will never see a ballgame

      There's a child being sold right now

      and if they could, they would swallow this

      pandemic whole

Bob Kaufman folded his

silence in neat squares

He was too 2-ply for this

world, he was the shit!

--Edward Vidaurre

Because Silence

I'm asking a question
and you just won't answer

I take another sip of wine and peer
into the other room

thinking you must have come in
without me knowing

I have heard that you like to hang around
between people's breath

or hide yourself on the avocados
I imagine you are my favorite color

the color of the spiky center
of a magenta flower

The same color that I last painted
my laundry room walls

and entrance way
I'm not sure if you even exist

but people seem to believe you do
either way it doesn't matter –

I am still watching for you
lifting my mask as I sip my wine

because silence seems to be
your only answer

--Khadija Anderson

Rainbow Seasons

My son tells me
it's rainbow weather. I see the drops
falling as the sun shines. He
is right; rainbows are born
from reflection. Something beautiful created
from what is opposite the sun. We are living
in a rainbow season now. I am in
my rainbow season. What is opposite the sun
when it is behind the clouds? Is it
still warm?

My womb releases all the dreams it now
will never carry. (*What are dreams anyway
but reflections, spectrums of light?*) I take advice
from her during this rainbow season,
when everything is change and talk of change,
when letting go is the catch term
on everyone's tongue, because it's what we have to do
ready or not. And reflection and release
and the warmth of the sun on our skin
and released dreams, like spectrums of light, shining.
Memories dazzlingly opposite our present and certainly
our future, a future which makes promises like goodbye kisses
in old black and white movies
where people said Bon Voyage to one another
and meant it. This.

This is what will get us through
these rainbow seasons.

– Amy L. Alley

Before Dawn

A stillness broken
before dawn,

in the name of
all that's hailed,

in the name of
our very present,

in the face of it all—
the remaining past

unclaimed, driven
forth by faith.

Waiting for news—
we are divided.

Spinning chaos into order,
death into birth.

Looking for an exit—trying
to recall a memory of you

in the great affliction
of time.

--David Dephy

Day of Heartsease

In summer the old round water faucet bubbles
      over the edge, flooding the lower garden.

This winter day I turn, look beyond the window
      at snow caught by bushes and trees.

A sparrow wings its way in the opposite direction
      of a drifting sunlit cloud.

Smoke sifts from the dull red chimney of the house
      across the street into nothing.

Adding its wishes, wind gently shakes shrubbery
      as if to wake it to the day.

My senses immerse in the scene's serenity as seen
      from the still of this room.

Yet my mind cannot avoid worries about the virus
      now stalking the world.

My hand casts a shadow moving larger than the life
      seeping on to this page.

--Wanita Zumbrunnen

Home at the End of the World

Silence on the streets
except the line jangling
on a dog's chain
--- we walk
as the crow
flies, certain
that nothing is certain.

Quarantine is not unlike
a previous life.
But in another world.
I -- infectious plague
I, the phony, the imposter
I -- full of self-doubt
waited for my failure
to be found out

Now I know
what paranoia prepared
me for.
A tickle in my throat
becomes a shame
that can't show its face
in public.
The wheeze in my chest
terrifies me
of the unknown,
a sickness
and a stillness...

So contradictory
the way the sands
shift beneath our feet.
The beauty of time, still and silent
--- ponytailed girls
play tennis in an empty
park, the three-legged dog
polices the yard
with his barks.

So peaceful,
the end of the world
--- and how long.
Hold me tight
and close.
Don't forget my name,
my love.
And know that fear
and freedom
are tricks of the mind.
How often one mistakes
flight
for dying.

—**Lauren S. Reynolds**

Pandemic Hygge

*Hygge: a quality of coziness and comfortable conviviality
that engenders a feeling of contentment or well-being
(regarded as a defining characteristic of Danish culture).*

Before, we were often out,
or if in, FOMO'ing
over things missed,
breakneck busy, awhirl.

Now, laptops humming,
side by side, we settle,
orange-scented candle,
hot, honeyed tea.

This scene could be
a lamp bright-lit
against night's dark,
each window a porthole

circled on the side of a ship,
a sweep of beams from
a lighthouse combing
over black water.

We tuck into couch,
blanketed by long hours,
try to wrap against
menace, invisible,

unbidden, the still
light scratch of the
lurker we know is
pacing just outside
the front door.

--Elline Lipkin

The Minnesota Smallpox Epidemic of 1924

& in that winter of outbreak most could not
prepare   especially not the poorer people
yet in the race for winners

of prizes/ equations blithely built on columns on
origins & ports & manifests in the unsteady
practice of progress

Kepler's mother's long ago arrested
for a witch & Leonardo writes backwards
& the Washington Monument's plumped & smoothed

set off in a distant great dismal swamp   &
Hugo Van deer Goes goes insane on a painter's
shoestring   after all

these exploits the melancholy rat man
arrives with a wild roving sigh
& a cloth over his head

openings cut for his eyes
to see through & protected by a long rubber
pestilence coat he lights your lamp grandfather-alien

& swarm & scour graceless erupts
new birthed from your mouth/ migrant/ stranger
intruder words like   *work hope dream*

eat save love   & a godforsaken
Slav tongue trips you on your way but the fever
of possibility

infects your blood/ bedrock/ fluid/ variola & all
the air's stuffed with rags   & some survive &
some do well

& others worse & sooner   or later
your children & grandchildren want to know
what came before the surname's shift/ terminus

shard   drift   husk   before
your blighted brilliance bruised your stars   *us*
          etiolate lights out

before your stymied ambition staggered you tailbone
to asshole to spine/ case-hardened
before

you tucked it safe into a pocket or your sock/ cradled
vestige   before your palms & soles
softened

you saved your shoes
in a cupboard all summer
but you don't go barefoot   anymore

--Mara Adamitz Scrupe

Regrets

Seven weeks ago we met together
Small hugs, bright smiles, pots of foods
Each of us from different places; beets,
Lasagna, strawberries, casserole, wine.
Our loud talk bounced from worlds
To planets, into hearts.
We made plans for the ceremony
To honor our new Poet Laureate,
Fussed over details until our eyes
Drooped and watered. Yet, we wanted
To stay together, work...early call...
That was the last time.

How I yearn for the sound of voices
As they vibrate the air into my ear.
How I wish for the shared meal,
The crazy talk, the planning.
How I want so badly that small hug,
The breath in the air, scent of food,
The kitchen mess to clean,
The silent replay of the evening.
How I yearn for my real people.

--Marlene Hitt

ii.
... seclusion

{March}

Deaths, March 1:   0
Deaths, March 31: 3,170

in just-
after e.e. cummings

in just-
sequestered spring   when the world is toilet-paper
manic the small
hobbled maskedman

wheezes   near   and far

and trumpandpence have
lost their marbles and
luscious loot and it's
sequestered spring

when the world is bottled water-awful

the queer
old maskedman wheezes
near   and   far
and nancyanddiane come dancing

from farkle and mexican trains and

it's
sequestered spring
and
    the

        cloven-hoofed

maskedMan   wheezes
far
and
near

--Mary Langer Thompson

The World Gets Quiet

Recently I received a letter referring to this time which we are all now sharing as "The Pause." The term caught my attention, and since I read that letter, I have seen it used a number of times. I feel it captures the essence of what is now taking place on our planet. These are indeed strange times. I find irony in the fact that each year large numbers of people die from tuberculosis, malaria, and the flu, but this pandemic brings us all together to a table of common concern. Its effects among the poor demonstrate that poverty is always the truest economic indicator.

It seems that our Earth is free, temporarily anyway, of the violent depredations we daily inflict upon it, and the results are immediately seen all over the world. These thoughts help me keep The Pause in perspective, and stay clear of the freaking-out response. I was in Death Valley the day before Governor Newsom called for the lockdown. Death Valley was pristine. I lay on the sand dunes reading my book and gazed up into the Panamint Mountains. Deep shadows, great wide alluvial fans, impossibly panoramic vistas. The imposing beauty of racing white clouds and towering thunderheads. The distance between myself and nature dissolved. I drove back to Los Angeles on empty roads.

On the drive I thought about growing up in New England, because the trip to the desert had somehow reminded me of that time. As a boy I lived outdoors. Zoomed everywhere on my three-speed bicycle. Rode to the coast to eat hot clams with tartar sauce while overlooking the Atlantic. Rode to the Concord River to go canoeing. Rode to Walden Pond and swung birches out over and into the water. In between adventures, I read so many books. When I read *Silent*

Spring, Rachel Carson captured my heart and my mind. As soon as I read her sentences, I knew I was reading truth. Her vision merged straight into my boyhood adventures and dreams. Her thinking seemed so natural; the idea of ecology seemed as real and as immediate as the snow on the blue spruce outside my window and the red cardinal singing in its boughs. "Those who contemplate the beauty of the earth find reserves of strength that will endure as long as life lasts. There is something infinitely healing in the repeated refrains of nature -- the assurance that dawn comes after night, and spring after winter," Carson wrote in *Silent Spring.* It made perfect sense to me.

Lately, I've been seeing pictures of the animals in Yosemite coming out to wander the campgrounds and hotels. Wild goats on the streets in Wales. Lions asleep on African roads. Now when I walk in the mornings, sometimes I see coyotes running down our streets. In the evenings the sky over the city has never been so clear. Each night I step outside onto the patio to stare up at bright planets and stars as if seeing them for the first time. Since we were told to shelter in place, temperatures have remained in the 70s; there has been steady on and off rain; gentle and pure or occasionally lashing and cold, but always welcome. The hills have been verdant, though summer is around the next corner. The daily beauty I see in these ordinary landscapes has been amplified, offering perspective.

This pandemic is being portrayed as a ruthless and unbending thing. But the pandemic is not the only enemy we need fear. The wild animals sallying forth, the crystal-clear skies, the deep azure waters are telling us something important about time; about the time in which we live; the times we have created. Many have now passed under the shadow of this virus. But many more, far more, have reemerged into the light. The larger issue is the way we have come to interact with the earth, with the animals and fellow human beings who inhabit it alongside us. The world cries out for a new ecology, a revision. Can we do that? It remains to be seen.

--Michael Haussler

Come Home

Come home, Earth said.
Listen to the songs, said the birds.
Look up, said the sky.
Watch our leaves in bud, said the trees.
Let me sit on your lap, said the dogs and cats.
Work together, said the ants.
Feel my touch, said the breeze.
See my light, said the sun at dawn.
Bring your chicks close, said the chickens.
Create new schools, said the fish.
Give thanks to the sand, said the shells.
Flow to the source, said the rivers.
Stand still, said the mountains.
Be slow and silent, said the turtles.
Let your bodies rest, said the stars.
Expand, our hearts said.

And we did.
And we did.
And we did.
And we did.

--Cassie Premo Steele

Teaching During COVID-19

I saw my high school students for the first time
about a week after the schools shut down
to curb the spread of COVID-19.

Seeing my students on Zoom and hearing
their voices, listening to their worries, laughter
and stories was so healing, even on a computer screen.

One of my students messaged me that both of her parents
and her brother lost their jobs.

The other day, a student messaged me from Honey Baked Ham,
where she is an essential worker, and said she can't make it
to Zoom class because she is working and is sending this
message during her 10-minute break.

My 12th grade student tells me that their year ended on March 13th,
the last day of school before closures. Others agree.
They miss being able to experience prom, graduation ceremony,
grad night in the same way as students in previous years.

Several students tell me that they are busy helping
to watch their younger siblings and helping them
with their school assignments.

I wonder how they can juggle so much.

We don't know how long this stay-at-home order will last.
The governor says through summer for sure. Perhaps through fall
and winter.

--Teresa Mei Chuc

Black, Indigenous, and More Writers of Color

I have visited various juvenile halls throughout Southern California to facilitate writing workshops with young men and women, the vast majority of those youth being of Black, Latinx, and Native American roots. Each time, during the brief time we shared together, I arrived with a commitment to create community with these young people, something worth pursuing, even as many of them were still just "in the middle" of a system with a vested interest in their incarceration and other forms of disenfranchisement benefitting from their poverty and limited access to resources.

The feeling invoked in me when these programs came to an end was always a conflicted one; on the one hand, I was happy to *see* the Black and Brown youth, even if just for a limited time, during which I sought to let them know that *they were seen* and not forgotten by their peers. On the other hand, when our program's funding came to an end, I couldn't help but feel like so much of our work was *only the beginning* of far more work to do for our collective freedom.

Today it's only more clear how as Black, Brown and Indigenous bodies, we shouldn't have to be seated inside of jail complexes guarded by chain-linked fences and barbed wire in order for us to speak at length, to write, and to visualize and thus determine our futures according to our own judgments and volition.

Today it's also clear that Americans need to set new standards for themselves if they're to create a lasting turning point during this historic time of the pandemic and the social justice protests in our communities. I hope it's become clearer for our society how violence pervades nearly every walk of life where ethnic communities are concerned, including due to policing, displacement, disinvestments in education, lack of decent, affordable housing, and more, all so that a handful of corporations can extend the economic engine that reproduces inequality, one generation after the next.

Apart from writing, I really love to read, especially the work of other Black, Latinx, and more writers of color and people with perspectives varying from the norm. But did you know that a 2019 survey conducted by Lee & Low Books shows that more than three-fourths of jobs in the publishing industry are held by White Americans, particular by predominantly straight, non-disabled White women? What kind of message does that send, especially to the brilliant Black & Brown youth like those we've seen?

The message is that while a multitude of voices exist in the most ethnically "diverse" country in the world, the industry is dominated by just one segment of the population, while Black, Brown, Latinx, Indigenous, queer, disabled, and more voices are left to occupy a tiny corner with one another. If that sounds like segregation more than 124 years after Plessy v. Ferguson's Separate but Equal decision from the U.S. Supreme Court, that's because it is.

As one commenter pointed out regarding the survey:

> *The issue concerns BIPOC and LGBT people not having an equal voice in an industry that shapes education and culture. Gatekeeping is real. Essentially, the survey results show that white cis women continue to have the loudest voices in the publishing industry and continue to decide which books should be read by the masses.*

My mind thinks back to the scores of young people I've met in Los Angeles, not only through its detention centers, but also at its inner-city schools, so many of whose tremendous voices can stun the world with reverberating effects. I want the world to know that not one Black, Brown or Indigenous writer anywhere should have to first be granted permission from overseers of detention facilities in order for us to speak and write with our communities; instead, we should be supported for doing these things in order to prevent more bodies from falling victim to the prison industrial complex and the pandemic. The publishing world also belongs to the Black & Brown, and various other marginalized communities, who have taught and affirmed me as a writer and advocate for arts and education.

And so, onward we continue.

--Jimmy Recinos

This essay first appeared in a prior version on the author's blog, *Jimbo Times*, June 24, 2020. It was originally titled "J.T.'s Publishing Platform will be Strictly for Voices from Black, Indigenous, and more Communities of Color."

Faith of a Seed

Her parents are downstairs cooking breakfast.
A lesson will begin soon.

She approaches her jewelry box
so she's presentable online.

She won't tell anyone her throat is scratchy
her forehead hot.

There lies the faux diamond her boyfriend bought her
last time she saw him in person.

And the wishbone charm,
a favorite from childhood.

She can't decide--
every necklace an amulet.

She picks up the smooth pearl black box
that holds the little mustard seed of faith.

The clasp is broken.
Maybe her father can fix it.

--Mary Langer Thompson

Los Pájaros Saben

Los pájaros saben
> They perch on wires looking down at me with sorrow

Los pájaros saben
> I whistle a tune, the kiskadee turns away

Los pájaros saben
> The moon is sliced in half, beyond the western skies

Los pájaros saben
> The mockingbirds orchestrate the shrill of a pandemic

Los pájaros saben
> The woodpecker's morse code is the answer

Los pájaros saben
> The nervousness in the way my wrists toss bird seed

Los pájaros saben
> They know of the dying clergymen in Italy & locusts in Oman

Los pájaros saben
> Why the river feels so familiar to drowning children

Los pájaros saben
> That a poet stands below them in search of words

--Edward Vidaurre

Cold Vivid State I

From the dome Governor Gavin proclaimed a statewide stay-at-
     home decree
The Sacramento measure spanned forth over fields and hillsides of
     every county,
City, and tiny town— east, west, south, and north—shutting non-
     essential markets,
Diners, and taverns down like a trunkless tree. So thrice a month of
     calendar days
Were dark like Monday Broadway plays: here were chains, grated
     gates, boards,
And locks where shops abound; closed, too, were churches with
     their holy halls
And sacred worship spaces, as were cash green theme parks and
     garden grounds.

And oh! The religious chasm which broke out and, supported by a
     godless crowd,
Shouted down the will of the greater common good. It was savage
     folly, yet as holy
A chant as ever under a rapidly waning harvest moon a married
     man was heard calling
His illicit lover's name out loud! But despite this chasm non-priority
     and commercial
Closings went on ceaselessly as libraries, malls, schools, shopping
     centers, and public
Places shuttered peacefully. Businesses and beaches south from
     Imperial Beach to the
Northernmost reach at Fort Dick cleared floors, chained parking
     lots, barred windows,
And locked store doors. As far as Chamber of Commerce grumbling
     about Big Brother
Went, Governor Gavin was a quick-study Man-of–the-Hour on
     the use of Sacramento

Scepter power: State recreation and sporting sites from the
   Redwoods and Yosemite
Inland beyond sulphur dead Salton Sea to the Calexico-Mexico
   border and the south-
Eastern California-Arizona state line along the Colorado River
   sandy cottonwood dales
And walking trails of Blythe to across the cliffs and petroglyphs of
   the wide Mojave.
Closed! For Newsom, not new come to leadership and keenly
   keeping score, heard
Scientists tout and reassure social distance as key weapon to stem
   pandemic horror.

                                        --GT Foster

My Students' Shoes

I try to walk in my students' shoes.
Stay there a while.
The one who is struggling,
whose mother is terminally sick.
The one who has a younger sister to take care of.
The student whose father is gone.
The student who wears the same black sweatshirt every day,
because that's his only one.
The student who asks if I have food,
because he's so hungry.
The student with tattered shoes so worn,
there are holes in them.
The student who loves to play the guitar
and often wears an Iron Maiden t-shirt.
So many pairs of shoes to walk in
while I am at home,
sitting in front of a computer screen,
teaching.

--Teresa Mei Chuc

Early Morning in Jamul*

Roosters crow wake up call
Turkeys gobble
Choir of dogs bark
Rabbits run for their lives
Squirrels scurry

Rain quench thirst of earth
Trees plants flowers colors pop
An oasis shades of green
Hail shines on cement *vereda*
Horses neigh

Bobcats coyotes mark their territory
Red tail hawks perform glide show
Sun blinks through gray clouds
Mountains watch listen
We walk talk let go laugh

Dog Chicha runs like lightning
Burrows into bushes
Hops jumps tries to catch butterflies
Tall grass wears raindrops
Ocean breeze comforts
Survival tap dances

--Gerda Govine Ituarte

---

*East County San Diego

Waiting It Out

In a dimmed-out living room
I can hear the rain outside
This goddamn virus
is making me feel sad

Staying home in self-isolation
depression is lurking in
Two long weeks cooped up inside
with only short visits to the garden

I try to tune out my feelings
and listen to the friendly rain
so I can keep at least mildly sane
till the virus can infect itself dead

--Martina Gallegos

No queda más que esperar

Desde mi sala un poco oscura
puedo escuchar la lluvia
Este virus maldito
me está entristeciendo

En casa, en auto-aislamiento
y la depresión presente se hace.
Dos largas semanas encerrada
con tan solo cortas visitas al jardín

Bloquear mis sentimientos trato
y escucho el ti-pi, ta-pa de la amistosa lluvia
para mi mente mantener lúcida
hasta que el virus, de muerte se infecte.

--Martina Gallegos

today I described seclusion

stillness
quiet
no motors
silent
clouds
breeze
no voices
son sits sheltered
daughter safe
in this rain
birds hide
is this non life?
popcorn
teakettle
I live
what shall I do now?

--Marlene Hitt

Pandemic Party

I am going to break away and
Have some fun
Before the damage is done
Enough television and radio
COVID-19 news coverage
When you focus on a problem
It does not go away
Whether you want it to or not

I will gather some Ruffles and avocado dip
Coca-Cola and Mello Yellow to sip
A dozen of my favorite CD's
Like Barry Manilow's first
Twenty or so of my most beloved DVD's
Like Marlon Brando in "On the Waterfront"
And dance, dance, dance till the sun comes up
Or the world ends

Maybe the media is making more of this
Than it is
Perhaps the sudden rules and regulations
Stuffed down my throat unconstitutionally
Have me doing the Disco Duck for luck

I just want some freedom
From the status quo
I am dying inside
And just want to live again
Free as a bird
Uncaged and uncuffed
I am a people person
Sitting in my apartment
By myself all day and night
Is but slow suicide

So, I am having a pandemic party
Without any local, state or federal government officials
If I get sick
I would rather have the coronavirus
Than the ache and agony of loneliness
The ruin and shame of a medical guess

--Radomir Vojtech Luza

Sunset Over Hahamongna

On weekday evenings during the lockdown, Ollie and I took five-minute drives from our house to the Arroyo Seco Watershed. After being indoors all day, it was nice to get out of the house and get some exercise and fresh air.

If the parking lot was closed, Ollie parked his SUV on a dead-end street overlooking the canyon. One of us stayed near the car, while the other walked a narrow trail that snaked along the rim of the canyon. From a marker I learned that Arroyo Seco is Spanish for "dry creek." Locally, it refers to the stream that begins in the San Gabriel Mountains. The surrounding foothills are named Hahamongna Watershed Park after a band of Tongva Indians who once settled there.

The foothills are not only habitats for humans, but for bobcat, gray fox, coyote, mountain lion, and deer. Mountain lions are rarely seen. But I imagined them creeping down mountain trails after dark when most people were inside. I imagined how peaceful it must have been years ago when the Tongva built their dwellings in the canyon, gathered fruits and herbs, and hunted deer and rabbit.

For us it was a scenic retreat from the constant bombardment of coronavirus news that was getting more and more depressing each day. Not to mention all the politically partisan mudslinging and misinformation that spread with the disease and news regarding the upcoming presidential election. Even if you didn't have COVID-19, the media frenzy was enough to make you sick.

I strolled on the trail with my trusted walking stick, resting my eyes on golden poppies, yarrow, and primrose emerging from the arid soil and gazing at wild chaparral cascading down slopes like a waterfall of evergreen. The scent of rosemary cleared cobwebs from my head, and peaceful songs of warblers, sparrows and turtle doves soothed my ears. If we were lucky, we'd see an urban cowboy riding his horse through the streets. The clippity-clop of the horse's hooves took me back to the old days before automobiles congested freeways, polluting the air.

The most spectacular part of the evening was sitting in the car watching the sun set in shades of gold, pink-purple, and blue over the mountains. It was a glorious sight to behold, making us feel further away from the ravages of the disease and maybe a little closer to God.

--Hazel Clayton Harrison

The New Normal

Why does it have to be
this way
this *NEW* normal

People have been
returning to life
as it was
but is it time
to do that

Here's the way I see it
this is another bump in the road
granted it's more like a
chasm than a bump

But many people in America
have had a lifetime of
problems
they never settled down
in order to survive
you learn to adapt

Why would you want to define
this with a slogan
if it is the new normal
why are so many yearning to
get back to yesterday

--RD Armstrong

Hunger:
Quarantine Day 17

I am so hungry. Not for meat or bones but for that wonder that we are wired for, the chest-to-chest embrace. In the church, we used to hug in greeting. In other groups, huggers emerged. How I have loved the sweet feeling of a child needing a little mama strength. Never will I forget Charlie, so willing to warm the moment with a giant man embrace.

How I wish for the arms of my sons, daughters, grandchildren. Like a plant without sunshine, I feel myself wilting, yellowing. Living alone in seclusion with only television and social media, I feel a part and apart. I read, write.

Knut Hamsun, a Norwegian author, wrote about the hunger of a starving young man who pretends to have an ordinary life as a respectable man. As his hunger increases, his reality, too, changes. He becomes delusional as he wanders darkly through the streets. This unnamed vagrant, an intellectual fellow, strolls in search of nourishment, becomes self-destructive and, without food, warmth, and basic comfort, his body begins to fail.

At one point he says:

> I suffered no pain, my hunger had taken the edge off; instead I felt pleasantly empty, untouched by everything around me and happy to be unseen by all. I put my legs up on a bench and leaned back, the best way to feel the true well-being of seclusion. There wasn't a cloud in my mind, nor did I feel any discomfort, and I hadn't a single unfulfilled desire or craving as far as my thought could reach. I lay with open eyes in a state of utter absence from myself and felt deliciously out of it.*

On which day of our pandemic self-isolation—with its message of saving others' lives—in this time of sacrifice, this empty time, this time of economic upheaval, will we begin to suffer no pain, become empty, happy to be unseen, comfortable with no comfort, craving nothing, not even the close embrace of another warm heartbeat? Like Knut Hamsen's young man. Maybe never.

I feel my hunger for physical closeness. In my dreams I banquet with those gone before me, those dreams filleted with sorrow.

--Marlene Hitt

---

*Knut Hamsun, *Hunger.*

I Hear Corona Calling

She says, *Hey, scared writer, you'd better unlock that drawer.*
Or I'll give you some heat, stuff your chest with regret,
cough your words out with sputum.
Credit me this gift of time to play
with your inner three-year-old
manuscript.

I recall a vision of reading from my poetry book
as listeners laud, *Your words mirror my words.*
Your courage stirs my courage.
Your pain frees my pain.

I take a step toward the drawer. The words are crying.
We can't live until you set us free. Only you have the key.
Don't be afraid to open us because we'll reveal your secrets.
You must be brave. Some may say STOP to protect their tender hearts.
They can't listen. They can't watch your pages unfurl because your words
open wounds, memories they've been hiding from, like you.

Just take us elsewhere or stick a label on us: for adults
willing to face their sadness and need us to push them through.
We won't take no for an answer. If you don't let us out,
we'll howl in your dreams and as you go about your day,
you'll hear us howling, stamping feet, demanding freedom.
We need to live, to share ourselves with whoever needs our words.

I take another step toward the drawer.
Knees shake against each other like boxers
packing punches for the knockout.
I put my head in my hands.
Raise my eyes, open the drawer.

Words fly out and circle the ceiling like tiny angels.
They clap and sing, *You and we are both free now.*
I lower my head again
and say, *Thank you, Corona.*

--Pauli Dutton

Everyday Heroes

Once, our local fields looked like the Mexican flag: green, white,
and red.
We could smell the rich strawberries along the 101
Freeway.
There's even a Strawberry Festival every late spring,
but the price of admission is now so high,
most fieldworkers can't afford to take their families,
and can only watch their hard work's results
from the other side of the fence,
their eyes fixed on all the strawberry wine, beer, ice cream, and
cakes.
They can see them; they can smell them; they picked and carried
the strawberries, but now they can't eat them.

That's how capitalism rewards their back-breaking work.
But they also reward them with cancerous pesticides
that ranchers spray around fieldworkers, even during their lunch
break.

Now many of these workers work the pot fields where
strawberries once thrived,
the rich smell of the fruit replaced by the stench of pot.
Farm bosses demand their workers keep working
during the Corona pandemic to feed the greed of America.
People still on the fields nearby fly higher than airplanes,
no license necessary.

Maybe this new, legal industry can create revenue
to provide roofs for the houseless,
the ones leaders forget or toss from here to there,
these everyday heroes exposing their health and families
to pesticides and now COVID-19,
these essential workers
keeping food on American tables
while their safety is put at risk,
these everyday heroes
and their sturdy hands that feed America.

--Martina Gallegos

Héroes de todos los días

Antes, nuestros campos lucían como la bandera mexicana: verde,
blanca y roja.
Podíamos oler las fresas ricas a lo largo de la autopista 101. Hasta
hay un Festival de las fresas ya para terminar la primavera, pero los
boletos de admisión son muy caros,
y a la mayoría de los campesinos no les alcanza para llevar a la
familia,
y lo único que les queda por hacer es mirar los resultados de su
labor
por el otro lado de la cerca,
sus ojos fijos sobre todos los postres de fresa: vino, cerveza, nieve,
helados y pasteles.
Los pueden mirar; los pueden oler; ellos las pizcaron y cargaron,
pero ahora no se las pueden comer.

Así es como el capitalismo recompensa la labor quiebra-espaldas
del campesino.
También los recompensan con las cancerosas pesticidas que los
rancheros
ordenan rociar alrededor de los campesinos, aún a la hora de su
almuerzo.

Muchos campesinos ahora trabajan en los campos de marijuana
donde antes las fresas florecían, el rico olor de fresas
ahora remplazado por el pútrido olor de marijuana.
Los rancheros exigen que los campesinos continúen trabajando
durante la pandemia del Corona, para alimentar la avaricia de
America.
La gente que aún trabaja en los campos cercanos, vuelan más altos
que aeroplanos,
licencia no requerida.

Quizá esta nueva empresa legal pueda crear ingresos
para proveer techos a los desamparados,
a quienes nuestros líderes lanzan para acá y para allá,
estos héroes de todos los días, exponiendo su salud y familias
a las pesticidas y ahora al COVID-19,
estos trabajadores esenciales
manteniendo alimentos sobre mesas Americanas
mientras su salud está en riesgo,
estos héroes de todos los días
y sus manos fuertes que alimentan America!

--Martina Gallegos

---

*Inspirado por mi amigo, Amadeo Sumano.   ¡Ánimo y adelante!

To The Mask Makers*
Bartels Hall

After using the handwashing station
and receiving a newly minted mask
and a Visitor tag,
I am let in to see inside
Cornell's glossy basketball arena, center court,
where in just a handful of days
you have made a difference:
a make-shift factory,
where daily more well-coordinated volunteers jump
to make new light blue masks, strong ones,
for health workers, those near the frontlines,
for vulnerable populations, for senior citizens
including me -- as asthma's my night visitor
-- for all who soon will learn to wear masks,
people and children,
we all who now need masks.

For how long, we may ask?
For as long as plague-bearing
Apollo of the far-shooting arrows
binds us in his sight,
his curved bow tight,
for as long as merciless Fates --
Clotho, Lachesis, and dread Atropos --
keep up their spin, apportion and cut us down,
just to remind us of how fragile we humans are,
our bodies, if not our spirits, worn thin by pandemic,
just so long,
that's how long we'll need masks.

And for this your team wisdom, strength, foresight,
dedication and resolve,
I thank you, my friend, and all you volunteers, I thank you
for making this year, this 2020 and COVID-19 and
the unbearable lightness of being
somehow more bearable.

--Carolyn Clark

---

* *Thank you, Cindy D., and all the volunteers who barely looked up from their work, while I came to see and reap for myself this amazing spectacle.*

You're Beautiful

to my daughter, Guinevere, a physician

You're beautiful because you went into Medicine to save people;
      you saw this coming from your studies of Infectious
      Diseases.
You're beautiful because you walk the COVID -19 floor;
      you could have left patient care and worked as a hospital
      administrator.
You're beautiful because you've made peace with face, hand and
      body coverings; you sat with me and explained the risks.
You're beautiful because you spoke of what was possible to give me
      something to cling to; you said: *If you cannot breathe, nothing*
      else matters.

You're beautiful because you asked about my mother, who's in a
      nursing home in Birmingham;
      you prayed for me before you induced the coma.
You're beautiful in that your husband needs you, yet you stayed
      until I was stable in the ICU;
      and you got the families to make meals for the ICU staff.
You're beautiful because you removed the tube and I can breathe;
      there is no necrosis, sepsis or brain injury.
You're beautiful because you brought me back, you saved my life;
      when I praise you, you say: *There are so many risking their*
      lives.

You're beautiful and the unsung hero of this terrible time;
      you've earned the shelter of the myths and goddesses of
      healing.

--Charlene Redick

Day 20: Shelter in Place

Black. The color of death.
Thick, heavy, black it is.
The pure sound of its presence
is soundless, fearsome silence.
Icy is the feel of his hand
on exposed fingers,
tasteless, the liquid he pours
to quench dryness.
Ancient death swims
deep into this earth,
into tunnels leading down,
into this mountain of promise.
Obey. Silently slip away. Look around.
Who would know in that blackness?
What do you see?

--Marlene Hitt

Entropy

Over the past four years
the government clown
has been spinning plates
like you might see in a circus
one guy running around
6 impossibly slender rods
trying to keep the crockery
up in the air

And the government clown
has been telling us outrageous lies
and he's got a lot of people
spellbound watching those plates spin

Meanwhile government goons and
fools are busy taking everything
that isn't nailed down and stashing
them in huge underground bunkers

But we the spellbound are slowly
catching on we're not that dumb
we hear the scuffling in the background
but the big gov clown tells us to
watch the plates those goddamned plates
See how they spin see how the light
bounces off the surface don't look away
You're helping to keep them spinning
no distractions please ignore what
you and pundits think is *really*
going on just keep watching the plates
Hypnotizing isn't it

Sooner or later the plates will come crashing
down and chaos will attempt to take over

but chaos may be too sick and tired to
get up and out of the house much less
start anything out on the streets

Even the gov clown will lose his bluster
and finally become another average Joe
overwhelmed by the realization that even
God can't keep plates up and spinning
forever

                              --RD Armstrong

Essential?

I heard the news today. O, joy! No work.
I can can the can of cans, and these *vats*
Can bubble without me. But horror dawns.
My supervisor taunts: "Liquor sales spike!"

A grog buy spike means brewing's essential?
When gun sales shoot up, arming's essential?
Glu' hits the ceiling, so pizza sales like
Grout or caulk or pot make some mart essential?!

I own, I groan, so I'm off to earn this home.
I owe, I owe, always off to work I go.
Now what no timepunch can know, dearest
Dr. Phar'cy (a half-part pair of wits)

Sides with Dr. Bricks -- who with the WHO will
Serve the needs of vaxx -- and start to bellow:
DON'T DRINK BLEACH STAY IN THE DARK WEB
DREAM IS A SHOPPING SPREE OF PPE GET IT!

--**Seven Dhar**

Panis Dominicus

inoculation or smallpox   dust settles
in a bone box & it's 1912's influenzic rage
or previously's roseate

onslaught/ eight cadavers entrails

swinging clasp hands circling hopping
weakening tumbling it's a danse macabre/ a legend/ ring around
ring
around   meanwhile a fatherless child/ an orphan

some poor little microcephalic
Zika baby cries maternal/ someone's always the virus's
favorite in this the muddle   this aphasia

or aphonia/ lost speak

is the diction of disease & damage all the terror played out
in my head in this Quaker city/ so much good
intention/ our daily bread/ Panis Dominicus of right-minded

talk/ so much goodness makes me nervous & the ditch
circumscribes
the fancy town center we rarely leave & outside the afflicted
tear beyond the moat for scraps of

the dream at the edge

a woman her head & purpled stillness dyed for blood red
breasts her sweet black-bearded baby
boy's in custody she says prison's

the dying wound/ the lash & abject while we sit
conjecturing in our folding lawn chairs
we wave our sparklers circling the fire pit &

it's New Year's
Eve in a Quaker city & we make our patterns of pitch
& mirth   & we look ahead   to better days

--Mara Adamitz Scrupe

The Mind Blender

1

she lies
in her home
hospital bed
for two years
now

my sister
has no choice
but
to dutifully wipe her
after a diaper change

she gives her
a soft white
tuna sandwich
and a paper cup
of juice to gulp

on good days
she'll reminisce
with her daughter's help
the miracle of reversing
her husband's vasectomy

she will want
to call her once
teenage girlfriend
and even me
to pray for her

sometimes my sis
needs to be spelled
long enough to
do their laundry
buy food and cigs

i sit on the sofa
across from her
as she harkens
to the silence
hears planes pass

i tell her she has
such good hearing
then she says
it's because she
doesn't see well anymore

when the dementia
gets to her
all she can do
is recall how
she was babysitting

lost her virginity
to the child's father
later nursing episodes
where she was trusted
to hide the big gun

in the pocket of her
nurse's outfit
but she wasn't allowed
to use the pressure cooker
those can explode

2

she remembers
a boyfriend she had
he was black
he loved the outdoors
it was forbidden

she wonders what
happened to the boy
who was taken away
can't quite place
his name

instead gazes out
until she is reminded
to take her medicine
in her hand, wash it down
gulping bottled water

my sister has spared me
the sight of
her insulin injections
bed changes
only calls or texts when

she wants me
to bring over a pizza
pick up her pills
and a package of
American Spirit turquoise

if the weather's good
we'll take Ginger
for a short W-A-L-K
so she can sniff
her boyfriend's pee

and talk to me
how she'll leave
half of everything
to me because she
doesn't want bad karma

as we reach
my gifted Cube
she slips me
a twenty for gas
i've learned not to say no

3

drive off
to my own rented house
where my daughter
and her husband
take turns making

breakfast for
each other
eggs, bacon
and dual cellphone
entertainment shared

while i sit
at my desktop laptop
surf for teaching jobs
YouTube videos
and burn CD's

they take off
dressed up to
Instagram portraits
of fashionable she
captured by muscular he

i continue to WeChat
my chinese fiancee
who sends me photos
and videos to edit
and masturbate to

since the government
won't let her back in
anytime soon during
this coronavirus crisis
isolating us

to her life of
outdoor strolls
wearing a
mask
to fetch cooking oil
from a milk crate

and my daily
case research
to mark the oncoming
curve that must flatten
before we can touch again

sleep together
arouse our bodies
to suck and fuck
to give thanks we desire
at this late age

to dream of growing
old in each other's company
travelling the United States
in a recreational vehicle
returning to our homestead

to fondly look back
at the passed
anticipate the visit
of possible grandchildren
from both sides

--Don Kingfisher Campbell

Holy Hands

In tunnels and funnels
Parks like Larks

Now is the time to pass the rhyme
With the help of our holy hands

Whether painting like Picasso
Writing like Hemingway
Or painting pictures made of poetry
Like Arthur Rimbaud

Satan begs us to lose our minds
During this lockdown

Unholy war against an unseen opponent
Battle for a beloved balance

Use the creativity God gave you
The imagination of John Lennon
Passion of Sylvia Plath

And soar like a falcon to the sea
Using flowery fingers
Blessed thumbs to while away the time

Learn an instrument
Write an opera
Beckon the soul

Hearken to the heart
Make love before you start
Be another Beethoven or Mozart
Pen a symphony at Kmart

Be one more Shakespeare or Tennessee Williams
And populate a play

But even when this nightmare ends
Do not ever again ignore
The artist in your being
The fire in your very wire
The heaven in your hell

                        --Radomir Vojtech Luza

The V That Marks Us

Birds of a feather, you and I, trading out *'feathers'* for lines criss-crossing cheeks and foreheads like roadways in AAA brochures, tracking journeys our bodies have trekked, earthbound and piercing clouds.

I see you walking by my house, back curved to ground, permed hair a gray corona shading the paper mask you wear, dented aluminum legs you push squeaking over cracks, trembling your twig body with each conquered step.

There is a V that marks us both: one etched deep between our eyes, you and me, birds of a feather, the ensconced frown our tribulations carved on us through six, seven, eight decades building nests for shaking beaks, eye-beads focused on our food and sheltering wings.

There is the other V, frightening our bones, invading homes: the V doctors intone as TVs show scores and scores of birds like us pushed on gurneys, breathing masks shaded by corona hair wired and scared.

The V that politicians tout to minimize our toll, the V that tells our deaths were near, that proves the air our bird-twig bodies occupied is not a chasm slicing generations off the Human map . . . the V counting us dispensable.

I see you and other birds, all of us masked, watching the ground we tremulously tread, seeking signs that our lives count, reaching for the unlined hands, scanning uncreased cheeks, telling our hearts these won't abscond. They will not forget.

--Thelma T. Reyna

iii.

. . . introspection

{April / May}

Deaths April 30:   60,966
Deaths May 31:   103,781

Today I Saw the Bodies, Lifted

Into a makeshift morgue.
Whose bodies I don't know.
The city is silent with its own sadness.
Sirens cough and are quiet.
Dogs surrender to the cold.
They look like women's bodies.
The body of Mary, mother of god, resting
In the same shroud they wrapped me in when I died.
Shroud that keeps you safe from flies,
and from flying too far away.
Today they showed us the bodies, lifted
in front of a camera.
Bodies made nameless by our imagining, made heavy with their fame.
The white veil wrapped around the neck, the cheekbones, the nose.
Their white, cloth-bound faces bright as boats, sliding into the river.
Whose nameless solitude now claims them?
Who owns that river? Whose bright boats were those?
Who traveled in them, and who took them away?
We will never know.

--Tresha Faye Haefner

My Doctor Calls

he wants to know
why I missed my last appointment
do I have a fever
shortness of breath
gastric distress
muscle spasms
dizziness
do I need to video conference

I want to ask the Doctor
are you watching sick people struggling to breathe
are you lacking respirators
hazmat suits
have your patients ever
blown crack vaped smoked cigarettes
what do you think about bio-engineering
have you watched a child die
do you know where the crows have gone

there are knitting groups
and book clubs on zoom
I want to say
how grateful I am
to sunbathe in the park
the duck families
are getting ready for their promenades
I take long walks
eat sushi for breakfast
make love every night

I thank you for your care

--Nancy Shiffrin

Cold Vivid State II

New York City's shadow of virus death
Bloated lobby fat on halfway measures
As the poor struggled for last-gasp breath
Protective gear stocks suddenly treasures.
'Mid national lack of best practice advice,
Scores of the new dead lie on beds of ice.

At rest the lost do not feel the chill or the fender shake
Or hear the idling muffled hum the rented reefer truck
Extemporaneous mobile morgue holding tanks make,
Nor do the pre-grave backlog of poor, brown, and black
In cold storage care if autopsies confirm COVID-19 cause.
Corpses in slumber can only deliver shivers of despair.

While Madame first woman and children without pause
Drank milk and ate pan dulce at a party well attended.
The savoury cake was by an Albanian bakery man made
And eaten after everyone had played and they had sung
The sad song of the Lost Lenore. But none could recall
All the words nor the score nor how it began or ended.
Though the music had verve, the song was not so long
As people content to flatten the curve in safe sweet home.

Yet, some say, but hey, there is no guaranteed sure way.
Resistance is pure American; to simply obey is to cower.
They harp a unity song in notes, loud, sharp, and sour and
Denounce nonessential closures as an over-reach of power.
But beware, beware those shifty eyes, that fake orange hair.
'Tis wise to despise for grand surprise is a booby-themed

Ring spun round him twice and a change on Election Day.
For he has been fed steroid dreams and crooked schemes,
Tasted Nine God nectar, and is now naked drunk on sway.

--GT Foster

At the Height of the Pandemic:
New York City, April 7

"People have no idea this is going on. It's like another world."
--Frank De Paolo*
In *TIME Magazine, June 1-8, 2020*

1.

a world populated by spacemen in white hazmat suits,
gloved, gowned, helmeted for journeys into the unknown, but
earthbound, their faces somber behind acrylic shields, eyes above
N-95's the only human touch

they move in solemn teams, three or four, their combat boots
enwrapped in white, their duty for 12 hours straight each day to
collect the city's dead from homes, hospitals, alleyways, sidewalks,
backlots, wherever selfish Death snipped lifelines, soon or late,
wherever Death intruded to snuff best-laid plans of mice and men
in brutal COVID days

soldiers gather frail remains, old or young, zip them gently into
body bags, gurney them to vans and trucks that wend from
borough to borough, unending caravans of guardsmen and military
troops fulfilling this duty of death, consoling survivors, plodding
through as 24 people die each hour, this wrenching April 7, then
for days and days and days

2.

many soldiers had never seen or touched a lifeless body, and none
had seen this many dead on all their combat tours abroad, even in
the thick of war, had not gathered and loaded so many human

115

beings stricken so swiftly, so many bodies stacked like cordwood in 100 refrigerated trailers lined like sentries in disaster morgues in parking lots

so many caskets in chapels and storage rooms never meant to store, so many gathered bodies, 24 nonstop hours of different shifts, different teams, 7 days a week, lifting, cradling, bagging, pushing, so, so many souls felled by virus, the collectors' harvesting so, so relentless and bruising

3.

mid-March birthed New York's crushing avalanche of corpses, the tsunami of souls, an unseen flood of loss swamping civic networks tending death-- funeral parlors, mortuaries, county morgues-- till frontline heroes of 9/11 swept in again like angels from their rebuilt lives to help gather their dead, . . . and as death tolls spread through the city like concentric circles of an atom bomb, over a thousand soldiers and government civilians stepped up, risking lives to touch, to hold, to carry

4.

NY-- pandemic epicenter of the world, heartbroken, bleeding, invaded once with 3.000 dead, invaded once again with 15,000 taken in 2 months, stealthy executions sans fire and explosions

numbers flashed for weeks on TV screens, scrolling larger with passing hours and days: the NY dead who lie where breaths expired and must be prepped for passing to the other side, while hundreds die alone, unclaimed, are placed in plain pine boxes and buried on Hart Island in pauper graves

5.

what else can mortals in combat boots and paramedic vans do but brace
their breaths and backs for this new war?
what else can their eyes do but stanch their tears to help mourning families
shed theirs?
what else can a city do but gather its dead and shepherd them to
resting places in dignity and respect?
what else can we proffer them, silent and gone, but unconditional care?

'we don't do this work for the dead,' the medical examiner says to
his crew each morning and night:
'we do it for the living'

--Thelma T. Reyna

---

*Frank De Paolo was Deputy Commissioner, NYC Forensics Operation, and in charge of these operations. *TIME*'s article was based on journalist W.J. Hennigan's month-long observations and interviews on-site as the frontline heroes described here accomplished their mission. This poem is based on Hennigan's article.

Stay-At-Home Decree

This stay- at- home
Decreed by the emperor and his men
Began as a release from work,
From the world, from
The people, their urgent voices,
All those needs.

Weeks have passed,
Loose ends bundled up,
Arranged closets, small spaces
In perfect order, excesses ready to donate.
I know the world is still out there
As I watch the many screens at home.
I have become virtual.

Day 25, I left the house,
Few on the road,
Drove into late spring's
Abundant beauty.
Home alone has been strange, as is
This quiet new world.
I am old now,
Was young in January.

Early days of stay-at-home
Had found me washed, dressed, Makeup
on, a thin layer of
Wrinkle cream that no one saw.
Tasks finished by noon.
Today I didn't make the bed.

Dishes wait piled in the sink.
I have ended being tidy.
No One is coming.

Does that matter?
The wash and wrinkle cream?
Eating from the stovetop pan for
Lack of dishes clean?
These days are all alike.
No one will know.

--Marlene Hitt

A Pleasant Walk to Asparagus Patch

My cell phone and glasses shoved
into my pouch, five-direction-colored,
yellow, the color of the center,
the hue of Chinese emperors' robes,
not allowed to Korean kings.

A pleasant walk to my backyard asparagus
patch, the first shoot burgundy tip on ground hog day.
A week later, five shoots if I count one curved
away from the sun, bent to dig back into soil.

Corona social distancing, no trip to grocery.
Three weeks, corner-wilted Romain leaves, one quarter
onion, one half Roma tomato, bare space in veggie bin
larger larger. Asparagus shoots in the sun. My mouth
waters. Twenty-three shoots today, five close to a span tall.

My pleasant walk to asparagus silent eloquence of
Stone Henge rocks, a basket and a knife
in my hand. A pleasant walk to asparagus in
metallic yellow of April sun. This shall not be
the beheading day.

Do not eat me. Do not dare eat me. Raw
or charcoal-grilled. Wuhan bats' manic laugh rings out of their
bodies stretched with bamboo skewers shaped into crosses,
stream through million human lungs, strobe
light five-direction colors, yellow, red, blue, black,
and white of the powers, principalities, and rulers of darkness.

--Maija Rhee Devine

Lares Love Poem #2

for Sarah, April 10, 2020

Intrepid wind
you ignite my house
I cannot slow you down:
pollen or Amazon or both
you keep delivering more and more
than I ever asked for.

Like children our needs keep
changing: today the printer
tomorrow the pond pump
yesterday more *One-a-Day*
vitamins to keep us strong.

Me? Sending masks and a thermometer
USPS overnight to Brooklyn,
where the city that never sleeps
is now a sensory-deprivation box
and my youngest child's on fire
as a coal that keeps reigniting,
her jet black hair unwinding,
a coiled staircase over the courtyard
in my dreams: moist and dark,
Rapunzel's ladder,
the only way out.

Prayers also winging, though
taking flight, angels land on
breast and breath and shoulder
to give each statistic
strength, hope, and human form.

--Carolyn Clark

Etching a Sketch

This is no painting or portrait
Still life or Salvador Dali number

It is the beginning of the beginning
A sketch before the real thing

An etching of the future
A sort of measurement of possibility

Transporting me away from the masks
Hand washing
Six foot social distancing

The two inches officials at
White House COVID press conferences
Stand away from each other

The sketching taking me to nirvana
My heaven
Our utopia

Away from hoarding in the supermarkets
Rudeness on highways and byways

And the indifferent difference on
Sidewalks and street corners

I sketch to learn more about
Myself and those around me

During these uncertain and confusing times
I etch to hang COVID-19 with its
Own tongue

Drown this pandemic in
Its own spit
Etching my sketch

--Radomir Vojtech Luza

Passover 2020

Play for me the saddest song.

Something Judaic that reminds me of bread, left unleavened.

All over the world today, people are about to die.

Animal trainers and car mechanics. Stand outside at sunrise,

memorize their faces. The feel of their invisible weight on the
planet.

They are in the ambulances and the ambulances are on their way

to the ships, which will turn them away.

You can pray to God, but he is busy hardening Pharaoh's heart,

preparing a redness of plague.

There is nothing we can do to stop it. The cities paint

blood on the doorways. Sacrificing so many lambs.

We are saying goodbye to the world we wanted to live in.

If it was gold. If it was glittering. If it was anything we wanted,

now it is gone.

The stranger has come. Looks us twice in the evil eye.

Shrivels the grapes. Spotlights the local news. You say we are
changing

the world, but the world is here to change us.

On the day you die, it will still be this way. The clouds are

fluid. Tonight I will boil eggs. I will eat of bitter herbs.

I will mix salt and water and pretend they are not my own tears.

I will watch Yul Brynner play Pharaoh on television,

and Charlton Heston play Moses.

I will pray that someone's heart be softened.

I will pray for an honesty I cannot name.

I will submerge myself in this sadness,

and cross through the salt of another red sea, listening

to the suspended waves crash

onto soldiers, who follow close behind.   —

--Tresha Faye Haefner

The 258,305* Who Died of Corona

Each took 25,000 breaths daily
human diet closest to that of a pig
walked 80,000 miles in their lifetime, long
       enough to wrap around the earth three times
ketchup was once used as medicine, hadn't they heard
of hydroxychloroquine, Lysol, Clorox bleach?
Sneezed with eyes shut, open-eyed blast not possible
stretched out, their intestines 30 feet long
most spent five years of their lives eating, triple
that during lockdown.
Corona wins: popcorn jumps through the air
       only three feet.
Human bodies, each of 10 trillion cells,
took the last of 25,000 breaths, satellited
into dreams of no taste no smells
leaving in their trails the hearts of their
loved ones mortar and pestled to powder.

--Maija Rhee Devine

---

*The number of the Corona death of the world as of 05/06/2020 per Center for Disease Control (CDC) Press Release.
Source of facts: *National Geographic*

COVID Dusky Death

Need not be Phi Beta Kappa nor *summa cum laude* to agree
Why mortality spike-strikes from this color-blind, microscopic
Virus hit harder on this country's black and brown and poor

Seek common conditions that speak beyond general front door
Like less Vitamin D in some blacks to starker, darker deficiencies:
Mental well-being, dental hygiene, household health and wealth

Gaps create state of high rates of untreated or undiagnosed obesity,
Blood pressure, diabetes, heart disease, and stroke among fatal host
Of underlying conditions common in black and brown penury folk

Insidiously at work beneath overlaying historical benign neglect
Lie compounded psychological, political, and economic effect of
Wide acceptance of black and brown lack of health, help, or hope
And gloom and doom acquiescence to mobs and the hanging rope

Perennial last hired first fired one given more work for less pay
Take home dark toned earn fifty-six cents to white man's dollar
And thank banks red-line mortgages for the neighborhood squalor:
Dense housing; inadequate space for social distance or even grace

Meantime, shelter-in-place, wear a mask, wash your hands, don't
Touch face, cover mouth if you cough, into elbow safely sneeze and,
If you can find them, pass the rubber gloves, meat, and Charmin,
please

                                                            --GT Foster

Strange Teacher

Death is a strange teacher
We learn to open doors with feet
And greet with elbows bumping
We learn how much we need
Messy cubicle mates
And winding Starbucks lines
We cast forgotten spells
With fluttering hands
To propel love
The requisite 6 feet apart
Older brains evolve
With fingertips on touch screens
Neighbors hang like laundry
From open windows
To join the courtyard chorus
We comfort kids beneath blanket forts
And aging parents through translucent panes
While waiting for death's
Next hard lesson

--Christine Reyna

COVID KonMarie

Stuck inside,
we are worrying,
moving the furniture,
cleaning the before
never-noticed cobwebs
hypotenusing triangles
at the corners of doors.

We are trying
to purge worry, sort
photos, attempt to tame
the mountain of what now
seems like useless mail.
Practice gratitude in
ways that won't make
our eyes roll.

Cocooning
is not the right word,
more like taking refuge,
wombed inside
the bleached walls
of our once fingerprint-
whorled home.

The week of Passover,
we bleach counters,
let ammonia be blood
on the doorframe,
chase *chametz* from the
cupboards, cup a palm
over the first-born,

to say, no, pass by,
we left out a full cup
to offer the stranger,
but this plague
is not welcome here.

--Elline Lipkin

Humans & 4 Walls

1.

They tried to warn folks—you have a 'lock down,' or a 'lock-down,' but then there's 'LOCKEDDOWN!'

Harshest shackles aren't iron, serrated steel, cop cuffs, or De Sade specials. 'Sheltering in place' is sometimes *misplaced* and devoid.

2.

Apt. 4C: Fourth-floor walk-up in the Bronx. Hallway dusk of broken bulbs, faded plastic scooter wheels-up by the patched-up door. Piled mail in urine corners, dusty and crushed with boot prints.

9 people.   2 bedrooms.   5 children.   2 in-laws.   1 wheelchair.   1 bath.

Zero jobs.

This fourth-floor math is cruel.

3.

PRE-DEMIC, as some folks call how it used to be, glistens brighter as the walls close in. The 4C predemic kids ran in the block, shot baskets, ogled girls on stoops, took swims in civic pools, hung out at Buster's snack stand by the loop, did study group, played ball at school.

4C predemic parents still had fourth-floor spats, at night when he dragged his tired gear through the thin-skinned door, his breath laden with beers, body worn from hammering, ears too tired for tattle-tales from his brood.

Then: when overburdened night, its shoulders slooped from the hurly-burly of teeming streets and human flesh compacted tighter than a balled-up fist and ear-rending cacophony of wheels and horns and sirens and bells and the city anguish of uncountable souls striving to survive . . . when overburdened night spread its massive arms and legs and torso over the bricks, steel, asphalt, and concrete bones of the Bronx . . . the chaos in 4C shut its lids and slept.

4.

Harshest shackles aren't iron, serrated steel, cop cuffs, or De Sade specials.
    They are warm flesh she used to kiss and hold: his hands, arms, legs.
        They are the prized blood coursing through her children's veins.
            They are the voice that used to sing her to sleep after their bodies conjoined in lust.

5.

They, the scientists, tried to warn us about 'LOCKEDDOWN'!
They raised their scholar hands in public spheres of logic, facts, and commitment to enlightening us and said *there's trouble ahead.*
Sheltering in place is not sheltered if your abuser is sheltering with you.

Indeed.
Novel virus, novel anything, is first-time everything.
Truth not lived before, not unfurled like the pristine silk it is, is absent and alien.
Boxing ourselves in the Bronx in 4 walls with a thin-skinned, often-kicked-in, door imprisons us all in one another's laps, close, suffocating.
Or LOCKEDDOWN with an abuser anywhere.

6.

Apt. 4C: Fourth-floor walk-up in the Bronx in pandemic times.
Thin-skinned door is too feeble to muffle moans, whimpers, grunts,
> *groans.*
Too timid to throw itself ajar and show the world its misery.
Too stunned when she turns the knob to flee outside and he yanks her back
> *inside.*

9 human beings. 3 generations. 1 abuser. 4 walls.
The math sunders the heart.

--Thelma T. Reyna

Bird Watching

Have you noticed lately that not even birds
congregate on phone wires anymore?

Remember how they used to flock together
singing their wild love songs?

Now they perch in pairs standing feet apart
It's been four weeks since we were ordered to stay

inside and distance ourselves when taking walks
The last time I saw my daughter I wanted to hug

her so badly. With tears in my eyes, I watched her
walk away

No one knows when the quarantine will end
No one knows when we'll be able to congregate

in churches and schools, or dance holding hands
In the meantime, I'll look to the skies and keep
my eyes on the birds.

--Hazel Clayton Harrison

Four Months

L.A. County extends 'safer at home' order...until at least May 15
Crime drops around the world as COVID-19 keeps people inside
Coronavirus: Extra $600 in California unemployment benefits
SoCal woman, 25, recovering from COVID-19 after coma, ICU
DEA donates masks to LA hospital
SoCal Easter weekend traditions shut down amid pandemic
Funeral via Zoom gives family closure amid pandemic
Boys and Girls Clubs in OC open to help kids of first responders
Boris Johnson makes 'very good progress' in London hospital
With more people home, LA increasing trash collection
LA County to require face coverings countywide starting April 15
Job opportunities emerge in SoCal amid coronavirus emergency*
But what matters to me most is you're 7,000 miles away in China
And governments are preventing us from travelling to each other
So we use our precious cell phones to WeChat our feelings
Through passionate words, provocative photos, emoting emojis
We have distant foreplay in live video exchanging motions
You encourage me and I stroke until I have to let go of the phone
I show you the results and you text Go wash up
Minutes later I send you a pic of the sweet-smelling wrinkled tissue
And wish you a good night's sleep while I get up to pour some
cereal and milk together in a bowl

--Don Kingfisher Campbell

---

*All 12 headlines above are in order of their appearance in the April 11
morning edition home page of the KABC 7 news website.

Lockdown, My Style

I've always preferred my own cooking anyway
its spices surprise even me.

Never liked to be alone even during the day
heavy traffic out my gate on Martin Luther King Way
magnet for door-to-door handlers pushing past
No trespassing. Now, dogs sniff, joggers pant by.

Research libraries closed, my historian spouse
hunkers in a lockdown he calls his *incarceration,*
me his *warden, forces 8 fruits, 8 vegetables
per day.* I get to keep my guy 24/7.

Writing, writing, I hardly see mutation to my routine,
except ordering grocery online. After not driving a month
anywhere, setting out on a grocery pick-up, he lights up:
I'm so excited to drive to Safeway.

Nudged by dwindling fresh veggies in my
fridge, I look up *dandelion greens.* Every part's
edible even roots. I knew it about Korean dandelions
from my childhood war years. Surprise! Yellow flower tempura!

True, being isolated from our 17-month-old granddaughter
living 15 minutes away shoot Corona spikes into my heart,
then I see the sadness for what it is—a gadget of self-love, my fear
of her memory of me fading. *Me, me, always me.*

God bless Netflix, archives of documentaries,
operas, an infinite ocean. Had sports on TV not sunk
into a black hole, my captive would've turned up his nose
at Korean *soaps, dramas*, I say, our new bonding journey.

--Maija Rhee Devine

How It Feels

Foggy sometimes, like those dreams
You slog through, never getting there.
Sometimes clear as the windowpane
That looks out at the world
you're no longer free to roam.

--Judy Bebelaar

Watching the World Pass in Plague-Time

I am the patient waking from being etherized upon a table. I may as well be splayed out immobile on my back, seeing shadows only, of what world there is on the other side of the curtain. My curtain is a picture window looking out at a 3-way intersection where people come and go, passing into their "the way it used to be." Moments like these repeat themselves, but none of them will happen again.

Walkers, runners, locals, adventurous one-time visitors, all converge out there on the sidewalk and pavement to people my view. Runners with slender legs in tight pants run past, then turn around and run across my view from the other direction. A dog appears, then a leash, then a woman in a clear vinyl coat against the chill. The woman raises her right arm, bends her nose into the sobaco, gives the armpit a sniff in full stride, raises the left arm, breathes in, keeps walking. Inside, my angelito negro shouts out, "How do they smell?" How not to freak out the neighbors: practice self-restraint.

Increased foot traffic outside is one sign of the times. The regulars are now augmented by anonymous visitors. I wonder where they've walked from? I've walked all these neighborhoods, so they're welcome, wherever they're from. (Pick up after your animal, please.) Another change: a social etiquette for plague-time, which takes shape in a long-distance street tango. Walkers approaching from down the block alert on their partner. They stare at each other, waiting to see if the distant oncoming walkers cross to the opposite side of the street. The end comes in a paso doble with averted eye contact.

In plague-time I see a threat to public health in the unmasked stranger. He's heading toward other helpless people to hang out at the corner. All of them need masks. Face masks announce how our times they are a'changin.' In the military, when I saw masked faces in Korean crowds, I felt even more foreign for noticing those ubiquitous masked faces and wondered, *Where have all the faces gone?* Outside my window, the first passerby wearing a mask comes like an exotic license plate spotted in highway bingo.

A big guy appears for the first time, heading purposefully downhill. He carries himself like he'd been someone's First Sergeant. In maskless mid-stride, Top straightens his back, raises his right fist chest high in a sixties Soul Brother GI greeting, doesn't snap a hand salute at the end. Still, that's an old soldier remembering a different path a different time saluting a ghost. Right on, brother.

White cap, black face mask, shiny white beard, the man's face is a spot, like his dog. I smile at the image and the beard waves from across the street. Turns out he hadn't meant it for me. The runner in the see-through top jogs into view on my side of the street opposite white beard. Today she sports skin-tight silver bottoms that hug her buttocks to the gratitude of an appreciative bearded mask who has stopped and turned to stare. The sports bra under the see-through top engenders less gratitude, I suppose.

One day the couple with the stroller aren't masked, but the next time, they are. Day after day the maskless runner in stretch pants, see-through top, and white earbuds passes, turns, and runs the other way. Around the same hour, the fellow with the dramatic white beard follows his spotted dog around the corner, neither wearing masks. It's OK for the dog.

The neighborhood coyote materializes out of the morning gloom and ducks into the neighbor's bushes across the street. Coming up the street, a face-masked woman unknowingly follows her dog toward the coyote. She'd probably freak out hearing a voice shout at her out of the gloom, if I called out to warn her of the coyote, so I don't, and she passes safely unaware.

Cinco de Mayo arrives and talk of "reopening" spreads fast throughout town. In Oklahoma and Michigan, face masks get people shot. Orange County hasn't gone that far, yet. Here on the block, in Pasadena, gradual as face masks appeared after the March 19 lockdown, on May 5, facemasks suddenly go missing all morning.

I keep a mask/no mask tote board in my head. On this particular day, a bundled walker grey in the predawn stillness resembles a Michelin man, but her long bob and maskless face make her out a she. Then the stretch-bottomed runner chugs uphill, still maskless.

A maskless couple turns to head north, border collie between them to herd them home safely. Four faces, no masks: 0 – 4. I go 0 for 6 before I see the first mask, a woman with a bun of grey hair. A maskless man riding an electric monowheel whizzes uphill. He wears a helmet for safety. 1 for 8. A white-haired woman coming down the street wears her mask under her chin. Half a point. She makes the turn-around and chugs up the hill, mask still under her chin, still half a point. Maskless white beard who used to look like a spot makes the tally 1 ½ to 9.

Ask not for whom the mask toll counts; it counts for all. Only 1 ½ points for masks. The bell tolls loud.

--Michael Sedano

Redbud Strong Perfume

Redbud strong perfume.
Pink dogwood.
Rose.
Pink azalea. White azalea.
Honeysuckle.
Wisteria on pine.
Magnolia.
Nandina red fruit.
Huckleberry vine.
Wisteria hanging in oak.
One leaf falls.
Holly. Holly.
Ivy.
White dogwood.
Honeysuckle again.
Oak hydrangeas popcorn joy.
Pink azalea next to fuchsia.
Red camellia.
More white dogwood.
Daffodil. Pansy.
One woman. Ear bud out.
Me. Ear bud out.
How you doin?
Good. How bout y'all?
Good.
Good.
Take care.
Y'all, too.
We are learning the language of bloom.

--Cassie Premo Steele

Dear Corona Virus

you infinitesimal speck
of nucleic acid in a protein coat
eternally multiplying robbing us of breath
television broadcasts dire numbers
millions sick military makes ships into hospitals
you mimic the common cold
plasma might hold the remedy
our President squabbles with scientists
nags us back to normal

I pull my silk scarf tight around my nose and mouth
venture out to market
security guards hand us sanitizer
forbid reusable bags
I stock up on apple juice
marvel at how quickly you
emptied shelves of toilet paper
we wait behind taped lines
stand six feet apart pay masked cashiers
panic will not make Chinese mustard available

neighborhood park
playground chained homeless camp on lawns
you took out
a fat brown brooding mallard hen
iridescent mates fussing above
turtles I watched give birth
lone baby egret escaped from a private zoo

yet I wake grateful
dust the top of my file cabinet
cherish my husband's Teddy Bear wearing my purple hat
guarding my lavender rose in its milk glass vase
photo of me at three

I caress a piece of meteorite
are you an evolutionary driver
come to eliminate the least fit
as asteroids extinguished dinosaurs

my 75th birthday
do I need to be re-educated
I did not want to write a poem for you
I will scrub the shower
I will not have cake

--Nancy Shiffrin

COVID-19 *Lares* Love Poem #6
for OPG

Consolidate!
So now old projects can be done?
No interruptions, visitors, visits,
no destinations, so few appointments.
Write books, poetry, read and erase
Imposed solitude of time and place.
Wear a mask, a persona,
but keeping one eye on heaven,
this Easter season feel no guilt
in rejoicing in nature,
more faith-filled than reason:

Look! From the window, over open field
the sleek fisher now streams away:
a dark, wave-like pulsing motion,
abandons stealth, leaps in slices from barn
to home to woods' edge.
This is no woodchuck lumbering
from old holes and rotten firewood
to dodge our axe.
No, it's a wild wave, a pulse in fresh snow,
dashing from where fox kits and fawns
flip night and day in play below
our neighboring, huge, iconic
broken-down barn-willow,
to race back and forth mown trails
to and fro to the frontlines: young poplars soon
bursting in leaf-song applause:
Stay! Stay! Stay the course!

--Carolyn Clark

Death Obtains

                :as seeds   barren of two decades' sparing
spawn

                :as rosemary clenched in suckling scale/
in veins' closed system

                :as dried bugs & mouse ribs/ an abandoned breast
pump in a shoe box

                :as choke knots/ writhing/ noosing/ periwinkle's
grip in a garden's beds

                :as emerald borer in leafless ash/ spiny in April's
flush & mantling

                :as fossil mosaic/ contagion/ a stone road's
shivering beneath the world

--Mara Adamitz Scrupe

The COV'

Is it just me or is it eerie that T once tweeted "cov-
fefe" as if a big id were getting ahead of a bigger
ego, reaching for COV-19-and-84? The *only* word he
coined, it's the *worst* he ever uttered -- except for
all the others. Understand, if I get quarantined
and pass away, it wasn't the disease that killed me.
It was likely the empTV. It was likely the doom
scrolling. It was likely the trips to the fridge and
FaceTime and the times I took Zoom to the loo
as if y'all couldn't see me when I could see all'a ya.
In Japan, when the tsunami struck Fukushima, in
the village of Otsuchi, many were lost, and Itaru
Sasaki, a man bereaved, fashioned a phone booth,
placed it in his garden, connected it to the wind,
and began to dial the dead. Soon people from
throughout the island lined up to make calls of their
own. It was not the first time Japan parted the veil
to tiptoe across a Bridge to the Spirit World. The mind
staggers to draw a comparison. Two years before, it
could hardly get worse than news from Taiji, "The Cove,"
site of Japan's annual mass cetacean slaughter in pools
of their own. For the dolphins, with bigger brains than
humans, such a morning must be impossible to fathom.
Now driven into a COV' of our own, with no one to call,
dial though we might, here we circle. We're as restless
as gov's that prep to destroy us to "save" us, as if we
were captives in a village in the American War on
Vietnam, awaiting some brilliant red dawn.

--Seven Dhar

148

Crystal Light of Crystal Mornings

Look at Madonna in her royal blue velvet,
bejeweled crown on her brow – see how
the air crystallizes into a gold lattice
of purity? Angels' wings flutter in the breeze.

The Lady of the Bright Mount sits still, with
the Divine Babe in her lap, crowned with jewels,
watching you – eyes, eyes, eyes – see all –
past, present, and future – oh, yes, they do –

"Stay at home," they say, stay still, wait
for the golden air to crystallize around you,
fill with the mystic codes of sunlight, pouring in,
transmitted at noon. All birds fall silent, in awe.

Breathe deeply. The diamond air
of sunlit days is lighter than
the feather-light heart – without
terror, without guilt, without grief –

Think of babies, unborn
think of children, lost
think of grandmas, alone –
The Judgment Day has come.

Look at Madonna, she cares.
Our Lady of Angels, Archangels.
She wrestled the demon to the ground.
The baby is safe in her arms.

Our Lady of Seraphim, Our Lady
of Diamond Light. You will pass the test,
protected by the Lady of Infinite Mercy.
Theotokos. The Majestic Mother of All.

Pod twoja obrone uciekamy się
święta Boża Rodzicielko. O, Pani nasza.
Orędowniczko nasza. Pośredniczko nasza,
Pocieszycielko nasza.

She changes the air into gold. Space fills
with the diamond vortex. Seraphim wings.
So still. Crystal Air of Crystal Mornings.
So still. Diamond Light. Gold Lattice of Dawn.

-- Maja Trochimczyk

NOTE: After Madonnas from the Norton Simon Museum and elsewhere. With a
Polish prayer: "We seek your protection, Holy Mother of God. Oh, our Lady. Our
Advocate. Our Mediator. Our Comforter."

Flattening the Curve

There are no beds left
they asked us to pick a partner

My partner will have to agree to have my body
piled on top of theirs, or vice versa

That's what the sound of death knocking on your door sounds like

Share your tubes and ventilator with me
let's breathe
let's breathe
let's breathe

Did I buy enough toilet paper?

Did I pay the light bill?

--Edward Vidaurre

Our Good Earth Rising

I'm thinking of the birds now,
the finches and juncos and sparrows,
calling, from tree to tree
to connect, lacing the sky.
I'm thinking of how,
as their feathered numbers shrink,
I listen more closely to their songs,
see them more clearly,
love them more dearly
as the hymn nine centuries old
tells us to pray.
And I do.

I'm thinking of the air now,
how I want to drink deeply
from this sky newly clean,
thinking how quiet the streets
now—no more distant rumble
of freeway roar.
And I do drink it in
and I pray.

I'm thinking of Venice,
the canal water clear now,
so clear you can see
in the dolomite green,
the swimming, swirling
life- seeking schools of fish,
even as the seas are spoiled.

Thinking of Italians singing
now from their balconies,
calling to one another
with the old loved songs,
loved even more dearly now.

And I'm thinking now of Apollo 8,
how Lovell, Borman and Anders
left earth for the moon in '68,
how that flight
was a leap of faith,
but they leapt.

Thinking of how their buddy,
Collins, calling out into the darkness
of space from Earth,
You are a go for TLI,
and how he wished now he'd said,
instead, *You can now slip*
the surly bonds of earth
and dance the sky.
I'm thinking the sky voyagers
must have heard his song
in their hearts.

I'm thinking of how
Anders took that picture,
of many, the only shot that worked,
now the image, universal,
of *our good earth* rising.

They saw clearly,
and called back to us,
all of us here,
on Christmas Eve,
And God called the dry land earth:
and the gathering of the waters
called He the seas:
and God saw that it was good.

And for a while then, we saw too.
And now we must see again,
more clearly, our home.

--Judy Bebelaar

Collins' words from the *Nova* documentary, "Apollo's Daring Mission,"
December 26, 2018.

To Screw the Queue

"Do not enter here. Enter over there."
The trail to Trader's Market
stretches onto the asphalt
where masked working men berate:

"Hey, where the hell ya think you're going?"
"In? Inside." "The queue starts outside the door!"
That mob? Why? Oh, the Thing, yeah, I see.
Then I resort toward the line without masking.

But I shuffle off this mere mortal coil
(the long queue winding into the carpark).
I moonwalk à la Michael until I'm in
only to be screamed at, "No mask, no service!"

"But the employed bandits at the door said
my bandana was a clean cloth
and," I implore, "should be quite enough!"
"Well, where is it?" "It must have fallen."

Then as security escorts,
I point out their social error
and say, "I just need a bag of those.
How about it?" "You want to get us closed?"

This is the *nunorml*? Well, I'll never shop
at Jo's unless I get a discount of five fingers
and some toes or want pumpkin-flavored
something-gross. They owe me.

Do not enter here. Go wait over there? What
kind of way is that to treat an aspiring hoarder?
Tell you one thing, I blame B.S. for folding in
the primary. Now the whole world feels the Bern.

--Seven Dhar

For the Minister of Loneliness

For Tracey Crouch, appointed in England in 2018

If I were given your title,
first, I'd take care of all the lonely Eleanor Rigbys
on your island
then fly to our USA,
the whole nation a Soledad Canyon
where there's an isolation epidemic
and people try to hoard love in bulk at Costco.

I'd separate out the chain smokers,
couch potatoes,
and those with heart disease
whom they say are already goners,
but not the writers who try to learn their stories,
and are not really lonely, only written that way.

In your new position, kumbaya, my Minister,
for I have no one else to talk to.
I'll be on my front porch in the boonies
looking like a sad sack
because I have insomnia and lie awake
between short dreams packed with untrue lovers.

Don't despair. I'm prepared
if you tell me there's nothing you can do.
Just come before I'm as desperate as your Richard Cory,
who put a bullet in his head.

                                        --Mary Langer Thompson

Sleepless in PANDEMIA

I can't sleep much these d a y s,

yet I'm tired and need to

I'm filled with strange   d r e a m s

that seem to be building a

miniseries of   g r i m   realities at every turn

In the morning, i let out the dogs

there's a yellow   h a z e

that floats in my town

A stick-to-your   s k i n   enfermedad

This   p a n d e m i c   has me thinking

Is there a   g o d

then i remember the stories

the poetry and prose of the

antepasados, the   f a i t h   of my abuela

the observation of nature's language

And I   b r e a t h e   in place

P a n d e m i a   V i r u s

We seem to be more together in this

                                   d i s t a n c e

158

This morning, the first flock of loros

made their way to the wires

above our house

C a n t a n d o

A grackle perched,

head lowered   at   a   distance

                              --Edward Vidaurre

Still Life

Still entwined. Time
passes as time does:

so much behind us,
a little less to go.

No easy ride: peace
can be vexing—what

we've left behind us
the sun dips down low.

--David Dephy

We Raise It: A Poem for Los Youngs

I know. It's not fair. It's been more than three months since
everything up and changed. Since then, nothing has changed.
Everything is still a mess. Home is stressful.

I know. Even if someone says otherwise, it still feels like there's
nowhere else to go. Even when we step out, everything is
weird. Strangers are stranger. It's not fun anymore.

I know. The *pupuserías* are not the same. The *panaderías* take forever
to get into. The burger joints aren't even there anymore. Our
pockets don't have enough to get much anyway.

I know. You didn't get to say goodbye to your friends. Everyone
knew this was the last year you'd get to see each other. Now
everyone is fighting. Everyone online is just insulting each other.

I know. Summer's coming up and there's no pool at the house. No
AC. Not enough fans. All the sockets are taken.

Family is stressful. Everyone says the same about how we'll get
through this. Doesn't feel like we're getting through.

And I know. It can't be long before some more riots pop off. Cops
killing Black people. Whites got no love. How are you supposed to
walk around when they can get you any minute. Racism's worse
than corona.

I know. Everyone online is just stressing. And if there's just one
more argument—

It's not fair. Everyone is scared. It's no love. Can't get any love.

I know it's like a war that's coming. It's dirty. But rules are rules.

If they hate us, gotta hate them back.

I know it feels this way. And I know it feels like it just stays this way.

I know it's not a time for promises. But this is not a promise.

This is just to let you know that through it all, you're still heard, still seen, and still our future.

To let you know that you got every right to be mad, like from the top of your lungs, ready to let it all out. We're mad with you. We're tired of the same old story, too.

But I know that you know. How if we get another day, we gotta take it.

So we raise it.

-- **Jimmy Recinos**

Dalian Play

A week after lockdown is lifted
People gather in the square
To kick a soccer ball around
Ride bicycles with training wheels
Or just walk together again

This afternoon a blonde doll
In a blue satin dress and
A pink eared white bunny
On all fours sit on a wooden
Park bench ready to eat

The girl with a pink hat
And blue surgical mask serves
Them slices of plastic pizza
Using a blue plastic shovel
To dish the yellow wedges

The doll falls ill at dinner
The girl places a packet of
Soft cotton cleansing wipes
As a pillow on the red scooter
Rolling as an ambulance

The girl in the pink hat gives
The doll mouth to mouth
While wearing the mask
The bunny at the bench
Doesn't want to eat anymore

Twitches its nose at the small
Boy sporting a black woolen
Ball cap and smaller blue mask
He tries and tries to get bunny
To chew on some faux bread

Meanwhile the doll rests
Eyes closed, her blue shoes
Tethered by a red ribbon
To her wrist dangle under
This nearby hospital bench

The boy comes to visit
Offers dolly a few pine nuts
As medicine for the virus
In what they have named
Wuhan Children's Hospital

--Don Kingfisher Campbell

Originally published in *The New Verse News* on April 6, 2020.
See www.TheNewVerseNews.blogspot.com

The Best Days of Our Lives

They called us essential workers. As police officers it made some sense, but my colleagues are I are Detectives. Still, they said, you sometimes go out into the field, interview people, serve warrants, make arrests occasionally, so you have to stay. Except they made us trade out suits and ties for our uniforms. So we sat at our desks in our police "blues," radios crackling, gun belts getting in the way, and had to still do our Detective thing.

Then they altered our schedules, temporarily they told us, so that now we had to work a part of the weekend. They told us it was just in case—just in case a cop in Patrol fell out, we could be grabbed to fill the gaps, even on weekends. Had any of our Patrol brothers and sisters fallen out? Would any of them get sick, out there on the front lines, still having to be first responders? We saw some of our civilian coworkers sent home, without knowing when they would be back. We were told little, as information was scarce. We were the government, and we were still trying to figure it out, make it work, and protect the public while protecting ourselves.

Cops are a familial, tightknit breed of "warriors," unused to having to socially distance, step back, and worry that something they do, something they catch, might be brought back home to harm loved ones. Cops can also be conservative, mistrustful of what we think is unwarranted fear, group overreaction, government overreach, or politicized agendas. We err on the side of caution, as we seek out the villains in the group. The police cringe as mayors and governors release criminals from jails and prisons, all in the name of their safety, while at the same time expecting us to chase down and arrest beachgoers and hikers. We watch the crime rate increase, along with the spread of conspiracy theories; tensions between cities, counties, and people; between right and left; between black, brown, white, republican and democrat. Who can be trusted? Which news is accurate? Which narrative will prevail, and what will be done with all of us?

We have a gallows humor few in the civilian world would understand or appreciate. We make cracks about catching the COVID, getting to stay home from work, or getting forced to quarantine in the "FEMA Camp" down by the Rose Bowl. We predict how many couples will break up or get divorced from all the time being forced to stay in close proximity to one another; or that domestic violence calls will surely spike. We talk about staying 6' away from criminals and tossing them our handcuffs so they can arrest themselves. We trade and compare our favorite conspiracy theories and QAnon videos, and some of us wonder, half-jokingly, if people who get shot are having "COVID-19" listed as their cause of death. We laugh about possibly being issued "radiation suits," and about all the different masks we keep getting issued, paper ones, the N95s, and now a heavy, black cloth one with the city logo on the front. Then we complain that one's too hot to wear, especially as the summer months near.

We keep forgetting that we can't sit down at our favorite restaurants, and decry our food getting cold, as we have to find places to eat. A favorite pastime is finding the Starbucks that's closest, and that's open, so that we can get that coffee that gives us so much joy.

Every scrap of news, information, rumor or gossip is collected and analyzed, discussed, and debated. New protocols and procedures are filtered down from the top, via email and section meeting, almost weekly. They put up a "fever station" inside the Grand Lobby of the police building. All employees entering the place must have their fever checked — 100 degrees or higher and you get sent home. Police cars are thoroughly sanitized, daily at first, then weekly, then we didn't know how often. As we enter our vehicles we wonder if the cleaning product vapors are safe to inhale.

We are amazed when we hear "war stories" from the Patrol officers about responding to death calls. Protocols have changed. Now they have to wait outside the convalescent hospitals and retirement centers, letting the paramedics and firemen go in first. If it's a confirmed COVID-related death, the cop has to suit up in PPE, go in, and document the death. How much longer will this go on? When can we go back to our old schedule and wear our suits and ties? When can we sit down at Chipotle and eat a hot meal, fresh off the assembly line? When will the bars open up so we can go out drinking again?

We look forward to projected "soft" opening dates — dates that might someday have special meaning to us, like "May 15th" or "June 1st." We start sympathizing with the protests over beach closures, and with those demanding reopening. After a while, we are numb to the news and statistics about coronavirus suffering and death, which has almost become abstract to us — police — who are so used to seeing death and suffering.

We just want it to be over. We want things to get back to normal. We want to get back to chasing bad guys and fighting crime. They say, however, that things will never go back to normal, that the trauma of this age will leave an indelible mark on the collective psyche and memory of our society as a whole. Maybe, but those of us in police work know different. Human nature has a weird way of processing, storing and reliving trauma, especially the shared kind.

The cops realize that, for us, whether there's a new normal, or a back-to-normal, the camaraderie that exists between us will provide a cushion for the memory of these hard days. We'll look back on the pandemic and the subsequent civil unrest with a mixed sense of survivor's guilt, and elation that we survived, much like the veterans of wars past. In the future, police will look upon their partners, coworkers, and the new breed of cops, mentally dividing them up by those who "were there," and those who "wouldn't understand." We'll almost look back on the pandemic with fond memories, thinking they might have been the best days of our lives.

--Victor Cass

I Am Just A Citizen

the voice of fear is a flimsy tourniquet
against the danger against the danger
children have stopped playing in the rain
their mothers their fathers cannot see their futures
will someone speak the drenched language ·
who will spill water from their tongue
mouth=to=mouth against all danger against all danger
refreshed & announcing

I am just a citizen
 (but I can heal the world)

I am just a citizen
 (but I can defend the children)

I am just a citizen
 (but I can grant their wishes)

the voice of paralysis is a one-sided broadcast
without complaint without complaint
heroes have limped a coward's retreat
their lovers their teachers cannot feel their power
will someone leap the hollow language
who will muscle daring into their leap
hand=to=hand resolving complaint resolving complaint
convinced & revealing

I am just a citizen
(but I honor conviction)

I am just a citizen (but
I sip revelation)

I am just a citizen
(but I live my intention)

we can find enemies anywhere where are the allies
dedicated to chumping fear & paralysis
we can find the danger anywhere where are the havens
draped with honeysuckle for food & wisdom
we can find gangrene anywhere where are the vitamins
spiked with helium for circulation & vision

we can find silhouettes anywhere
where are the citizens where are the citizens
the voice of bravery is a chant of lightning
freezing the mirage freezing the mirage
heroes are charting the quicksand
their footprints their trailmarks
harden into muddy architecture
will someone stride with common purpose
who will gather to inspect the promise of oasis

voice=to=voice claiming the mirage claiming the mirage
honored & rejoicing

we are the company of the citizens we
are the company of the citizens we
are the company of the citizens

-- Peter J. Harris

Originally published in *The Global Citizen*, a textbook for first-year students
at Chapman College, Orange, CA, in1998.

For Whom Do We Mourn?

In this pandemic, for whom do we mourn? For ourselves, our old way of life? For the freedoms we've lost? The freedom to go to restaurants and movies, or hang out with friends? Or for the thousands of lives that have been lost to the deadly coronavirus? We hear of bodies stacked up in morgues like sacks of grain, and of family members who are unable to be with their loved ones in their final hour.

At times I find myself crying uncontrollably. I wonder if I am losing my mind. Then I realize that I cannot help but be affected by the rising death toll. Yesterday, tears formed in my eyes as I read obituaries of people that have succumbed to this devastating disease. Wilson Jerman, the son of a North Carolina farm worker, dropped out of high school to work on his father's farm. In his twenties, he moved to Washington D.C., where he was hired by the Eisenhower administration as a White House cleaner. From there he rose to become a butler, a prestigious job at the time for a young colored man without a college degree. After serving 11 presidents, he retired. At the age of 91, he passed away from COVID-19.

Roy Horn dreamed of working with exotic animals when he was a boy. He realized his dream when he became part of the dynamic duo of Siegfried and Roy. Years ago, Roy survived a severe neck wound from a tiger attack, but it was the claws of COVID-19 that dealt him a fatal blow.

The jazz legend Ellis Marsalis died at the age of 85 from COVID-19. He will be missed by his famous sons, trumpeter Wynton Marsalis and saxophonist, Branford, and the rest of his family. Mexican singer, songwriter, and actor Oscar Chavez, one of Mexico's best- known protest singers, died from COVID-19 at the age of 85.

In Santa Clara, California, Azhar Ahrabi, an immigrant from the Middle East, made daily rounds to check on neighbors, often befriending them with hot cups of her Turkish coffee. Her neighbors say they miss her sweet smile.

Julia Alexander, a former schoolteacher and public administrator, retired to pursue her dream of traveling the world. With her daughter, she had traveled to China, Brazil, Australia, and had cruised the Mediterranean, gazing at the South of France from a riverboat. She contracted the virus at a skier's convention. Her daughter watched her die on a nurse's iPad.

The death toll continues to rise. As of today, May 27, the virus has claimed over 100,000 American lives, more than were killed in the decades-long Vietnam War. There may never be a wall listing all people who died in this pandemic, but let us not turn our eyes away. Let us remember the pandemic victims and honor the contributions they made to society. They were ordinary people and extraordinary people, like you and me.

For whom do we mourn? We mourn for thee.

--Hazel Clayton Harrison

Memorial Day

I listen to Bach Cello Suites
low throbbing sounds a long sob
become the woman waving
good-bye to her mother struggling
to breathe behind protective glass
doctors try to heal the afflicted
without respirators with
increased oxygen piped into ICUs

we mourn soldiers lost in battle
we mourn COVID-19 dead
I recall my own incurable sorrow
best friend's corpse
ice cold in steaming heat
turning green turning blue
rigor mortis come and gone
doberman snarling at officers
how it grieved me to leave this
uncut pet crying for his owner

I learn about pandemics
365 new infectious diseases since Y2K
most passed from animals to humans
as wilderness becomes "civilization"
will we forever live in a masked world
will we never again assemble
will vaccinations be required

Douglas Park
a new duck family promenades
the children want to take them home
we talk and read and watch TV
grateful to pray for *Tikkun Olam*
repair of the fallen world

--Nancy Shiffrin

iv.
...realization

{June/July}

Deaths June 30:   126,140
Deaths July 31:   154,320

Say This Isn't the End*

... say we live on, say we'll forget the masks

that kept us from dying from the invisible,

but say we won't ever forget the invisible

masks we realized we had been wearing most

our lives, disguising ourselves from

each other. Say we won't veil ourselves again,

that our souls will keep breathing timelessly,

that we won't return to clocking our lives

with lists and appointments. Say we'll keep

our days errant as sun showers,   impulsive

as a star's falling. Say this isn't our end   ...

... say I'll get to be as thrilled as a boy spinning

again in my barber's chair, tell him how

I'd missed his winged scissors chirping

away my shaggy hair eclipsing my eyes,

his warm clouds of foam, the sharp love

of his razor's tender strokes on my beard.

Say I'll get more chances to say more than

thanks, Shirley at the checkout line, praise

her turquoise jewelry, her son in photos

taped to her register, dare to ask about

her throat cancer. Say this isn't her end ...

... say my mother's cloudy eyes won't die

from the goodbye kiss I last gave her, say

that wasn't our final goodbye, nor will we

be stranded behind a quarantine window

trying to see our refracted faces beyond

the glare, read our lips, press the warmth

of our palms to the cold glass. Say I won't

be kept from her bedside to listen to her

last words, that we'll have years to speak

of the decades of our unspoken love that

separated us. Say this isn't how we'll end   ...

... say all the restaurant chairs will get back

on their feet, that we'll all sit for another

lifetime of savoring all we had never fully

savored: the server as poet reciting flavors

not on the menu, the candlelight flicker

as appetizer, friends' spicy gossip and rich,

saucy laughter, sharing entrées of memories

no longer six feet apart, our beloved's lips

as velvety as the wine, the dessert served sweet

in their eyes. Say this is no one's end …

… say my husband and I will keep on honing

our home cooking together, find new recipes

for love in the kitchen: our kisses and tears

while dicing onions, eggs cracking in tune

to Aretha's croon, dancing as we heat up

the oven. Say we'll never stop feasting on

the taste of our stories, sweet or sour, but

say our table will never be set for just one,

say neither of us dies, many more *Cheers!*

to our good health. Say we will never end …

… say we'll all still take the time we once

needed to walk alone and gently through

our neighborhoods, keep noticing the Zen

of anthills and sidewalk cracks blossoming

weeds, of yappy dogs and silent swing sets

rusting in backyards, of neat hedges hiding

mansions and scruffy lawns of boarded-up

homes. Say we won't forget our seeing

that every kind of life is a life worth living,

worth saving. Say this is nobody's end ...

... or say this will be my end, say the loving

hands of gloved, gowned angels risking their

lives to save mine won't be able to keep me

here. Say this is the last breath

of my last poem, will of my last thoughts:

I've witnessed massive swarms of fireflies

grace my garden like never before, drawn

to the air cleansed of our arrogant greed,

their glow a flashback to the time before

us, omen of Earth without us, a reminder

we're never immune to nature. I say this

might be the end we've always   needed

to begin again. I say this may be the end

to let us hope to heal, to evolve, reach

the stars. Again I'll say: heal, evolve, reach

and become the stars that became us —

whether or not this is or is not our end.

--Richard Blanco

---

*Originally published in *The Atlantic,* June 7, 2020. Blanco was President Obama's U.S. Inaugural Poet in 2013.

This Poem Is Not a Prayer

This poem cries on an empty street corner in blind daylight.

This poem doesn't want a helping hand for fear of contamination.

This poem loves isolation, but despises the box she's confined to.

This poem listens to finches, when they stop singing, she awaits a
murder of crows.

This poem doesn't want wide-eyed strangers to feel sorry for her, to
tilt their heads as if they cared about what's between the lines.

This poem wears an N-95 mask over her nose and mouth. The mask
stolen from a young buck.

This poem plays pandemic drinking games.

This poem is not a prayer.

This poem sits six feet away from you, maybe six miles to be safe.

This poem wears a tattered dress over bruised knees, her torn
white-stockinged feet stuffed into scuffed black patent leather
shoes.

This poem washes her hands while singing Happy Birthday to Me,
Happy Birthday to Me, Happy Birthday Dear Dirty Hands, Happy
Birthday to Me. Estas son las mañanitas.

This brackish green brown poem lives in a muddy pond, deaf to
bird calls, she is indifferent to the lily eaten by golden frogs.

This poem continues to cry alone, laughs when told touching is a thing of the past.

This poem says goodbye too many times and wonders when she may take your blue hand.

This poem dies with you.

-- **Melinda Palacio**

The Last Butterfly

Some tried to warn us. Few
listened, until… until the
last butterfly crawled the
distance between leaf and
flower,
wings congealed in a bloody
mass, deformed
by our own misguided design.

Few listened, until
the last bird
fell from the sky.
Song silent,
blackened wings, useless
now, unable
to fly.

Few listened, until the
last baby
nursed on poisoned milk,
uttered a feeble
cry
and left us.

Too late
we listened.
Too late we
wept.

--Judie Rae

"Make America Great Again"-- A Man-Made Disaster

1

Secretive beautiful exotic
in the way you gaze at and caress
the face of your victims
spike-kisses of betrayal

stealthy legions boring into eyes
flooding nostrils
bold restless capricious virus
in the depths of the throat you
freely surf cell to cell
explode exponentially
hook into unsuspecting hosts
airborne again you charm and lance
another lover

2

Via eyes nose mouth corona arrives
invisible infectious exterminator
fever chills dry cough
fluids fill lungs
struggle for breath
trachea intubation
oxygen eases desperation
midazolam arises a long sleep
outside family members
anguish unknown future in
"The Greatest Country in the World"

3

COVID-19 plague downplayed
a cacophony of misinformation untruths
exaggerations nonsensical suppositions
dizzying conjectures offered by
highest political officials in DC:

"It's a hoax!"
"We have this virus under control, almost airtight."
"It will miraculously disappear, soon it will be
down to zero."
"We have tested the most of any country!"
"Anybody can have a test."
"I see the disinfectant that knocks
it out in a minute, one minute."
> *"And is there a way we can do*
> *something like that by injection*
> *inside, or almost a cleaning?"*
". . .this is a great success story."

like colorful computer images
of coronavirus weak pitiful attempts
at happy talk to paint a pretty picture of
the man-made disaster that screams:
"Make America Great Again!"

--Alejandro Morales

Momma, Momma

(last words spoken by George Floyd)

Finally watched the video
had to write something
to ease the ancestral pain in my soul

We

       Kneel to pray
       Kneel to profess love
       Kneel to tie child's shoe
       Kneel to show respect
       Kneel to protest

Police officer
       Presses knee on neck
       New weapon of choice

George Floyd: I can't breathe
Police officer: Get up and get in the car
George Floyd: I can't breathe I will I can't move
       Momma Momma
Police officer: Resisting arrest   You can't win

Witnesses yell
       His nose is bleeding
       He's not resisting arrest
       How long are you going to hold him down
       Now you have a baton

I tell my husband what I wrote   break down in tears
two words hang in my heart   *Momma Momma*
a child's cry for help   *Momma Momma*
a man's cry for help as he suffocates to death

           --**Gerda Govine Ituarte**

8 Minutes, 46 Seconds on 38th & Chicago

When my ex-husband, Kevin, and I moved to Minneapolis in the mid-1970s with our five-year-old daughter, we were refugees escaping the racism and bigotry of the Deep South. After graduating with a business degree, Kevin had accepted a supervisory job with an agricultural shipping company in Baton Rouge, Louisiana. We had both lived in Ohio for most of our lives, and I was apprehensive about moving South, but job opportunities were scarce in Ohio, and I was determined to make the best of the relocation. When Kevin's life was threatened by White employees because he tried to transfer some Black workers out of the hazardous grain bins and replace them with White workers, I knew it was time to leave.

I'll never forget the note he found in his locker. Written on yellow note paper in large block letters were the words:

NIGGER GO HOME OR YOU'LL BE ALLIGATOR BAIT.

I'd had enough. I convinced Kevin to request a transfer. Within a few weeks, we arrived in South Minneapolis, a few blocks away from the now-infamous corner of East 38th Street and Chicago Avenue.

Back then Minneapolis was a friendly place, welcoming Black emigrants from the South. Even in working-class neighborhoods, streets were pristine with small corner stores and restaurants. There was little crime, and we walked unharassed through quiet, elm-tree-lined streets. Demographically, the city was less than one percent Black. We missed our Black culture, but assimilated as much as possible. I was hired by the State in an administrative job. We learned to eat gefilte fish and sauerkraut and to speak with a clipped Midwestern accent. We strolled beside limpid lavender lakes in summer and watched locals ice skate on their frozen surfaces in winter. What a liberating feeling it was! We felt free. Well, almost.

Fast forward to May 27, 2020. I am living in the Los Angeles area. There is a familiar sickening, gut-wrenching feeling in the pit of my stomach as I watch on TV the video of the May 25 lynching of an unarmed Black man in Minneapolis on the corner of 38th and Chicago, the same corner I used to walk by every day. The man's name is George Floyd. He lies prone on the pavement, both hands cuffed behind his back while a cop presses a knee into his neck and two others pin him down with the full weight of their bodies. Another cop stands guard daring the gathering crowd to interfere with this brutal, unconscionable murder in broad daylight. As the video recorded by 17-year-old Darnella Frazier rolls, George's voice can be heard crying out, "I can't breathe! Momma! They're gonna kill me."

For eight minutes and 46 seconds, the cop pressed his knee into George Floyd's neck. It was the longest eight minutes and 46 seconds I've ever lived. Watching the callous look in the cop's eyes, hearing George's pleas, I felt helpless, shaken to my core. His cries for his momma still ring in my ears.

When a child cries for his mother, the mother instinctively runs to his aid. She embraces and comforts him. George could have been my son. How many mothers have stood by helplessly and watched their children lynched, murdered, executed by a racist system that devalues black lives? Emmett Till. Eric Garner. Michael Brown. Trayvon Martin. Sandra Bland. Ahmaud Arbery. Breonna Taylor. Thousands. And in all of the senseless killings, America turned a blind eye!

I was 11 years old in 1963 when Addie Mae Collins, Cynthia Wesley, Carole Robertson, and Carol Denise McNair were killed   in the 16ᵗʰ Street Baptist Church bombing in Birmingham, Alabama. In 1965 I watched protesters beaten, hosed, kicked, spat upon in the Selma to Montgomery, Alabama march. I remember the riots in 1968 in the aftermath of Dr. Martin Luther King, Jr.'s assassination, and I witnessed the 1992 riots in Los Angeles after the cops who beat Rodney King were acquitted.

Standing in my living room feeling sick and disgusted after watching the video, I did not know this time would be any different. The protests started that night on the corner of 38ᵗʰ and Chicago. Despite the coronavirus lockdown, men, women, children of all colors stood on that corner, pumped their fists, and yelled, "BLACK LIVES MATTER." They finally understood that more deadly than the coronavirus, racism had been killing black bodies for over four-hundred years.

Some of the protesters looted and burned the 3rd precinct, but the majority were peaceful. By the next day, protests had spread to Chicago, New York, Cleveland, Atlanta, Los Angeles—all of the major cities in the U.S.A. Soon after, protesters marched in London, Paris, Capetown, Hong Kong, Tokyo, and many other cities all over the world.

Though my aching feet would not allow me to take to the streets, I stood up and cheered, picked up my pen, and began to write stories about this historic movement. Black lives matter! George Floyd mattered. All people who have suffered and died from the knee of white racism and oppression matter.

--Hazel Clayton Harrison

God Is

I

God is an open wound. A kung-fu movie and a celestial sicario. God
made our president with leftover road cotton and grackle
droppings. His sandals are of leftover human skin from the factory
of suicide rock stars. Today he wears the knee caps of Janis to match
his ufo belt. God is unfazed at 3 pm. He whispers to me from a six-
feet distance. God lies naked on steel surfaces with his long hair
covering the shadow of men. God has a sticker on his chest that
reads, "I voted."

He's nonchalant. He has a twin. She does all the good work.

II

God is your god's God, yoga and breathing, she is the breath of life,
latex gloves and exhaling the sun over mountains, she is the
blamed, the curve, the torn achilles heel, God is a beat poet, the
coming strain, the big question, the control, the last-minute mind
changer, the finger on the gun, the safety switch. God is the
ultimate filter, the event planner, the street cleaner, the thing in the
sky that was there and then was not, the ventilator, the death toll.

She knows the bodies are coming.

III

God is language, a lisp and stutter, God has Down Syndrome, the
autistic genius, the only child, from the other side of the
tracks. Have you ever thought of God as old? The wrinkled hobo
and toothless smoker, the girl next door, the square-jawed bad
hombre, creator of a new earth between ellipses, growing peonies

on hyphens, God is soil and water. The trans angel, the monk making booze, the anorexic gargoyle breaking off a ledge, the movement in the painting. God's number is eight digits behind iron bars, the noise maker, the vuvuzela in purgatory, guilty!

God is doing time.

IV

God is a found poem, in exile, an unbelievable truth, an asteroid belt crash, mammoth, THAT sound, THAT silence.

V

G o d is tired of rising on Easter. G o d is trying to figure out the diameter of this pandemic, writing ghostly hymns for the dead. Did you not know G o d was the celestial laureate? Skywritings, the sounds you hear in the morning, of birds and wind chimes, speeding cars and barking dogs, did you think the sound was just that? Commotion? G o d writes those sounds into existence every day. I know when G o d is in a Motown mood, a hippie rock, or just a lounging jazz mood, and when it's too quiet… G o d let the whiskey get the better of him.

VI

God likes to drink with me. I listen.

--Edward Vidaurre

Questions

Texas
a woman is jailed for reopening her nail salon
she would not apologize to the judge
she has to feed her children
her employees have to pay their rent

so much TV ya ya
what the president says
what the scientists say
what the governors say
what about that lab in wuhan
what about the live meat markets
what about genetic engineering

neighborhood park
yesterday a masked boy harassed the ducklings
struggling to climb out of the pond
stomped his feet waved at them threatening
interrupted Mother's promenade
not many last an on-looker tells me
usually predators take the weakest ones

a girl lifts a turtle out of the water
mockingbirds congregate on the lawns
aren't you frightened a woman asks
where are the crows

--Nancy Shiffrin

Summer – Speed and Steed

Summer flashes by like a firefly
lighting a small space of time,
always moving towards fall

as if days are runners in a race,
and I, an excited child, tumble
in one somersault after another.

Summer is a herd of deer startled
into racing across open land
to the cool recess of a thicket

where their soft brown eyes meld
into branches and twigs, as suddenly
still as their flight is swift.

Circulating blood moves faster
and faster through my fingers
giving rein to the steed I ride

heedlessly on summer's carousel
in constant forward movement up
and down, and upon dismounting,

arrive at fall, having spun dizzily
through space, clinging insect-like
to a steed racing at summer speed.

--Wanita Zumbrunnen

Something

This has something to do with the *tap tap tap* of an early morning
dream,
with traffic rushing by and people who talk too much
and jet exhaust and red-tailed hawks.
This has something to do with plum blossoms every February
And then hard rain.

This has something to do with the curve of future plans,
with Esalen, Constantinople, Positano, the French Riviera,
with trips that may never be made and hope gone awry.
This has something to do with fires, full lunar eclipses,
and sudden gusts of wind blowing down fifty-year-old elms.
This has something to do with nests falling out of trees.

This has something to do with swimming all the way to the raft,
and lying on hot wood with silty water drying on your skin,
a hand flung over your eyes to keep out the sun,
something to do with wars and babies,
with uterine cancer
and a nice calm game of draw poker.
This has something to do with birthdays
and friends, and just-missed trains,

something to do with cedar and spring bamboo,
with the shades of green and yellow in a sun-struck cornfield,
with the gaze directed at the horizon and balance.
This has something to do with moss between stones,
with blue between patches of clouds,
the moment between inhale and exhale,
with how John died that beautiful June,
and with how improbable it was that I met you
because of a broken hinge on a broken door
now the door to our bedroom
made lovely by your hands.

This has something to do with how I still miss him,
especially on June days when the sky is clear to the west,
with how wrong it was that he should die at only 49,
tall and strong and loving the ocean almost more than me.
And this has something to do with my love for you.

--Judy Bebelaar

Originally published in *Schuuylkill Valley Journal of the Arts*, 2007, *The Widows' Handbook, 2014)*

There

I don't want to struggle with this invitation to a state
where it's inevitable I'll hear the sound of my childhood nickname
slip from the lips of a fairly elected leader

where I can bow my head at the end of an ethical life
& be honored with a necklace strung with jewels
compressed from the voices of Paul Robeson Billy Eckstine Peabo
Bryson
sparkling in the facets echoes of Sunday quartets
content with round-the-way praise

my last visit will be vaccination against social viciousness
when I raise my head in thanks jewels will jiggle on wire
& click against each other & everybody at the homecoming
hears their favorite songs ringing my neck

guards in such a place move like rejuvenated Pips
their weapons on safety
highlights of my whole life
sung into the lethal end of rifle barrels

show me where grown folk get down
 where power & humility shine on sober faces
                    there be decisive as sunlight
I won't struggle with this beckoning
I will not stutter when it's time for me to pass it on

                                        --Peter J. Harris

For Every Working-Class Father and Mother

On this Father's Day--during this most critical year for our nation--I hope it's only becoming clearer that if our nation has respect for the concept of the family, then it should *show that respect* in its treatment of families everywhere by uplifting them, as Kobe "Bean" Bryant was celebrated for uplifting his daughter Gianna Bryant.

In the days and months following the untimely passing of this first-class pair, the city of Los Angeles, along with people all over America, mourned their sudden loss with many words, moments of silence, and testimonials. Though it may seem just a faint memory now, one can still recall that in the short time before the coronavirus, almost every other day in L.A. was marked by some kind of space for mourning the unthinkable loss of the Bryants and other families above the hills in Calabasas.

Today, mothers and fathers, in the wake of George Floyd's killing, march to protest the preventable deaths of their sons and daughters--or those who could be their family members-- at the hands of law enforcement's excessive violence. The parents and all the other millions of marchers since Floyd's death protesting police brutality and social injustice are participating in collective grieving such as what arose for the far more famous Bryant family not long ago.

But every human life, no matter how rich or how poor, is absolutely worth fighting for, and worth demanding a better world for, as so much of the working-class is calling for, once again, in America. When state and public officials choose to meet such vital demands with indifference, force, or disdain, they are openly betraying--once again--one of the ideals they claim to want to uphold. Hence why we mourn, Los Angeles, and why we must continue to rise again.

The battle is long. But it is still our duty to win. Kobe Bryant knew this. And that's why we loved him. Or at least, why we claimed to. The time has now come to extend that love to people just as human as Bryant and his 13-year-old daughter.

We march for justice.

-- **Jimmy Recinos**

Wreaths of Garlic

The Israelites in the wilderness
longed for the garlic of Egypt,
but I have *The Stinking Rose* of Gilroy.

I was afraid my purchase would
rid my vehicle of New Car Smell,
but the college girl offered to double-wrap it.

The herb had no sacred power that day.
Did the clove lose its clout to ward off evil,
demons, and *la maldad*?

Perhaps we need to start wearing garlands
or smear broken bits on windows and doors
for fertility and magic protection of our hearts.

Let's hang braids in birthing and sickrooms,
swags in kitchens, and serve it generously
to our families to lower our blood pressure.

Let's chew cloves before entering battlefields
and before our night journeys
to conjure dreams of something we lost long ago.

Let's breathe the scent again, even as we scatter seeds
among pandemic graves and hang wreaths on each locked door
where grief resides.

--Mary Langer Thompson

Outbreak

isolated like a prisoner in his hunkered space,
the ticking clock, the television's unblinking eye
watching him circle his apartment, his death row place
to quarantine for fourteen days, to remember and cry
about the party with dancing, laughing, her lips upon his face

the first week of solitude left him aching for family affection,
he read the papers and scrolled the news across online sites
that gave confusion and death rates from COVID-19 detections,
he sunk deeper beneath the repeated stats and national spikes,
the endless waiting and furloughed days offered little direction

as voices thundered like protest clouds on the streets below,
he saw hundreds who marched and shouted out names
of Black men and women caught within a vicious flow
of victims smothered beneath racist systems of shame,
the stolen lives and dreams of those he would never know

when the doctor delivered him and eased him into the sun,
he hungered to be a different man than who he was before,
seeking a new world, he pledged to justice yet to be done,
the brutal deaths that videos flashed he could no longer ignore,
his activism would be a weapon for all to breathe once more

--Mel Donalson

Wreaking Happiness Against a Weaponized Pandemic

"What did he pretend to be? A prophet. A shaman. Motivated extraordinarily, thus extraordinarily motivating. Taking the same drugs they took, which he himself provided. Though of course he didn't actually take them." [William Gibson, The Peripheral, pgs. 282-283].

"The study of happiness never was a luxury to be postponed until more serene, peaceful times. ... From earliest times, views of human happiness have been set forth against the background of suffering, poverty, disease, and the inevitability of death." [Sissela Bok, Exploring Happiness: From Aristotle to Brain Science, pgs. 5 and 6].

Old Black people used to tell us: be twice as better than the average white person to get just as far

Our elders ... experienced prophets divining future under ! Oval Office man-child !

George Clinton for President is no more absurd than surreal life in the time of an Emperor Wanna... ... be Jim Jones on steroids ...

believe this spotlight hog this unchecked waste of blood bone and breath this president of Petty Mediocrity Enterprises
     ['we suck at everything but theft of the public trust, feudal demands for loyalty, one-note denials, blame gaming, and credit claiming']

drink whatever concoction's gargled by this enemy of the state whose every step is a crime against humanity and the exploited staff at gold-plated shitholes

remain vulnerable once more to the unvanquished virus that's poisoned us since Thomas Jefferson wrote that 'all men' are endowed with the 'unalienable' right to pursue happiness except the people he legally owned and sold to pay off his debts

I remain a card-carrying member of the
Dozens Institute of Southeast D.C., Richard Pryor Division

Paging Dr. Funkenstein
Shine your laserlight

/// through havoc bleeding from incoherent blah blah blah ///

... Spend tax dollars on e pluribus unum ...

lead us as we lift every voice and sing:

whitelessness is volunteer asphyxiation
willful innocence
groove-free allegiance to a one-click life
See No Evil, Hear No Evil, Speak No Evil on layaway

I am my elders' ambassador
to all hard-working citizens and true public servants

thank goodness, years ago, I pledged my allegiance
to One Nation Under a Groove!

Wreaking Happiness during a weaponized pandemic?

break this fever with joyful citizenship against the Okie Doke in the spirit of Marley's One Love *Out of many, one?* essential, interdependent heavy lifting ahead, seekers or as Stevie Wonder sang

You'll cause your own country to fall!

--Peter J. Harris

Bringing Her Home

in honor of Susan Rae

The photo says it all.
The young woman carries
her grandmother's
ashes, cradles the urn
in her arms as she walks
past silent neighbors
waving their goodbyes.

Not the ending we wanted
for her, no memorial
to honor her, though she
remains memorialized
in our hearts: her quick
laugh, her love of children,
her witticisms.

To end like this,
no family or friends
at her side allowed to say
our in-person good-byes
allowed to kiss the sweet
face that remains now,
in memory, she but one
victim of the mysterious
plague that roams the earth.

She would rail
at the unfairness

of it all, not for
herself, but for the lost,
the poor, the loved ones
denied a hand to hold
at these last moments,
denied one final, poignant
farewell.

--Judie Rae

Sempervirens

Last night, in my dream, crystal wine glasses,
showers of them, spilling down,
into a bottomless well,
their shattering soundless.
And that image in the book,
The Overstory, about the souls of trees
and of people. I've been reading it
to distract me from that feeling
of fought-off despair.

The image of the broken
young man in a wheelchair
stuck in a muddy rut. Looking up,
he sees the *Sempervirens*,
the towering tree he sought,
its shaggy red trunk just ahead on the forest trail,
a triple wide door of darkness in the side of night.
I put the book down on the bedside table, oak,
beside the carved wooden box
that holds the pill I forgot to take
to prevent a crippling stroke.

I fell asleep in the quiet forest
and woke again in our bed,
to the buzzing, anxious dark.
Maybe it's just these days, the heavy fog
of helplessness weighing us down.
Or maybe memories of last night,
my husband filling the kitchen
with angry arrows, all aimed at me,
I thought, or maybe my own anger,
pushed down, or maybe at the man
with the strange pompadour
and his endless *fantastic* in the midst of a crisis
he can't seem to see.

And now this morning, gloomy still,
and still last night's anger
hanging in the silence,
as we drink coffee.
Then it condenses as words,
bitterly dripping from both of us.
Then silence again.
But he takes my hug, at first stiffly,
then returns it, gives in a little,
letting one arm linger around my shoulders
and goes out.
Soon, the hammer's *crack crack crack*
as he works on the new back stairs
and the sharp clean smell of the new cedar shingles
reminds me of what I should have said instead.
Now *I* feel like the mean one.

Last week the back door opened
to a three-foot drop, dirt clods
and piles of lumber.
He just kept going out to work,
knowing exactly what screw or nail,
which tool —
maybe a marlin spike,
maybe a drift.
Exactly what's level
and plumb
and what's not.

I envy him, wish I had his steady way.
I hesitate, procrastinate,
and when I finally face it and try,
I can't make up my mind.
Which thing is both like and unlike?
Which word has the right tension, right sound?

How many thousands of times
have I clicked on *tools/thesaurus*?

How many hours spent online
looking for a bird, for abracadabra,
for the names of clouds, dark matter,
for our current scourge?

Too often, I've given up, put it on the back burner,
stored everything in the Dropbox
where poetry lives
and poems die from neglect.

But as the power saw whirls and whines,
I think maybe I'll try hammering away
at what's impossible to say.
Maybe I'll drop some wine glasses
down the well, listen for the shatter
and the echo. Maybe I'll plumb
my awkward wobbles, my anger.
After all, it's Semicolon Day.
Why not connect?
Maybe I'll wheelchair into the woods of night.
Maybe I'll throw my cassock down,
get out of the rut,
and find the big tree.

--Judy Bebelaar

My Stone City

I walked you to sleep

on a Sunday afternoon.

Did you know you were dying?

There was no way to save you

for the trees cried kill

along the quarry of death

and the stones moved

and the green moss waited

and is waiting still.

I had to keep asking

how do you like it

and how do you like it

as you moved with me

up the cliff without answers

and over railroad tracks

I walked better than you

and scattered your bones

through the valley

and stacked your hair

in the barn

while your words escaped

over houses you never knew.

I had a hard time

crossing the creek.

It was young and deep

and you were riding on my shoulders

and I was tired

but could not stop

and I left you there

smiling at spring flowers

in unseeing sleep.

Left your stone heart sleeping

and kept walking, walking

away from your touch

and waking, waking.

--Wanita Zumbrunnen

Supposed To

You were supposed to get my pearls when I
died, and ruby-studded bracelets nestled
in the cherry armoire lined with silk, the one I'd
brought from Rome to someday will to you.

You were supposed to get my golden watch, mother's
wedding ring she left for me, and Mama Fina's velvet
box of antique photos we adored— treasures small
and big, things speaking to your soul.

You were supposed to read my decorated card, me
not propped in bed with limping breath, but gifting in
advance, sitting at your side, dear sister, basking
in the radiance of your eyes.

But gods weave plots without consent, marking
spit and blood on unsuspecting hearts, sending
unseen ghouls with microscopic crowns to blindside
us at rest, at play, entwined in arms, tending others.

Gods twist calendars and clocks to block
the maps of best-laid plans, sledgehammer us to
dust, stifling breath, shredding lungs, pilfering loved
ones with carte blanche.

You were supposed to outlive me, my angel girl, to
hold my hand in my last breaths, not fight for yours
in ICU alone, not slip away so soon like wisps of cloud,
frayed apart, piece by piece, like threads.

--Thelma T. Reyna

Here I Am
(a poem about love in the time of corona)

When we were young (not Gen X, menopausal, divorced, single mothers), we
Gathered in bedrooms and basements to sing at the top of our lungs

And when my wife spiked a fever, and I did an hour later, and I wondered
Who to turn to (the night had not yet gone, the night had not yet gone away)

I texted you: Girl. We have fevers. And you wrote back: Me, too. Call you?
(Doesn't seem that long.) Your voice again in the midst of it, crisis like seventh grade

You said you'd meet your doctor in a parking lot in the morning and we promised
To call our lesbian gyno in the morning (we have the right, you know. We have to right

To know.) You always believed in me and I don't know what caused me
To reach out to you (So much here is hard to lose) but maybe it was that

Morning you came over and sat on our back porch and we drank watermelon
Drinks and you said, Feel that breeze. See those birds. Look where you've

Ended up (and the cup was almost empty, but we toasted anyway and
You said to the woman I love: You see in her what I saw in her and I love

You (love is everywhere. I know it is) for loving her like this. And maybe it is
All up to you (it's all up to you) but here I am (the one that you love)

In so many ways (revolution, evolution, election, propagation, creation)
Tell me we can stay (tell me we can stay home, please) because these

Are the only words I can believe. We put on masks and gloves and cannot
Even sing (hold me in your arms. I promise this one will go slow.)

Because it doesn't. It comes out of nowhere like a gun shot, an axe, a bullet,
And that's how you know you have it. The violence of it (we have the right

You know). Asking for another day. Understand. In so many ways.
I don't know what to say. I don't know what to say. Here I am.

--Cassie Premo Steele

Motel Mate

Light washes over me at 6:43 a.m.
Like my mother's love
Father's paranoia
Sister's envy
Ex-brother-in-law's soft hands and weak demands

The sun in its
Orange neon heat

The coronavirus kicker
COVID-19 licker
Pandemic fixer

Murdering eight strains of corona circling the globe
Strangling them in their sweat
Stomping them like an MMA bet

As in "The War of the Worlds"
Where the virus dies on its own
Heat is our best friend
Sunrays poisoning the virus into retreat
Dead on its feet

--Radomir Vojtech Luza

Grit & Grief

for my dear friend

Unwavering strength woven into her curls her own pandemic
from within invisible invader could not get out of chair
ravaged enemies threaten to steal life away power of poetry
reflect and resurrect words to enter to impact to heal

They soothe sounds of now she inhales living while shadows
gather she thinks about those gone who still whisper in her ears
and hold a tender space only she can fill this woman gifts us
the magic of *morements* with those who love her without script

For them keeping her close is the only option as she nourishes us
from a distance without arms to hold kisses to plant hands to
entwine unable to gather at birth birthdays graduation funerals
even when tears flood their eyes smiles and laughter show up

She appears in sunrise sunset clouds because we know where
to find her spirit words come calling find her know they will be
honored she thinks about those gone hold a tender space
as she walks on high wire with grit and grief between her teeth

--Gerda Govine Ituarte

Reopening

orange monarchs light the daisies
honeysuckle permeates an atmosphere
once drenched with gasoline fumes
I breathe more deeply
never has jacaranda looked so bright
a partial reopening is official

we may go to the beach to
surf swim or bicycle
we may not sit on the sand to sunbathe
will there be another spike in COVID cases
why does the United States have so many deaths
do we keep the vulnerable alive longer
the elderly with pneumonia
babies with deformed hearts
addicts whose nervous systems have quit

the children don't understand
why the mother duck doesn't
want them to play with the ducklings
I want to browse in a bookstore
I want to use the library
curbside delivery is all that's available

I am grateful
to connect an electronic reader

--Nancy Shiffrin

Standing in the Forget-Me-Nots at the Hospice Window

I knew your dying would be more than I could take without this virus that now has me staked in this flower bed of forget-me-nots outside your hospice window. What kept me near was the thought that we could break the sadness down and you would go out with a smile, while I stayed, and joined you on another day. We're accustomed to talking through barricades, for we never had each other; we had poetry and we loved from far away; that was enough in a way.

The masked caregiver lifts the window and says: *Fifteen minutes and please stay six feet away.*

How are you? I call out to you.

You lie back on your pillow, swollen with lung obstruction—the seesaw wheezing, the nasal trembling, the grunting with effort--dazed and in pain in this warehouse of dying people where comfort is a forfeiture, connection a bane.

Rough.

I, in my stadium chair, look for anything to hold on to, because I know your kidneys continue failing at full tilt. You talk to me with your eyes. *Lily of the Valley* you called me with a lilt at the height of our lyric days, but now breathing comes very hard with long pauses and your focus on my face.

Better to exit with the virus' assist than stay on with so much amiss.

Your grin is a last-ditch effort. You are barely whispering now. *The Dying Room* you called this place on the day they brought you here. I smile wanly that poetry still serves you. You always saw the humor in the fear.

Ants and crickets are at my feet as I stand at the threshold of the afterlife and hand you a tiny nosegay of forget-me-nots, blue and sweet. Traffic speeds by -- masked people sheltering in place at their steering wheels. The sky changes colors. The world turns. More have died of COVID-19 than in the Vietnam War. Over one million cases in the United States.

In Wuhan, the relics of martyrs –five hundred ash decanters a day—are distributed by the crematoriums. During the war, the Japanese airdropped infected rat fleas to propagate Bubonic plague. A century before, the U.S. Calvary gave smallpox-contaminated blankets to Native Americans. Leper colonies in medieval times quarantined victims in monasteries. Before HIV was brought under control through a cocktail of drugs, 35.4 million people died of AIDS-related illnesses.

All these civilizations burned the bodies of these plagues. Will that be our lot? Not even a touch to know that you are cold, gone?

You glance warily at the death van across the street as it revs up its generators.

Air conditioning before the delivery into Hell!

Tears fill my eyes. I brace up.

You brought me heaven.

You push an envelope along the windowsill: several poems I've not seen. You are strangulating now, staying alive for me.

Close your eyes. Let go. This is no life, I say.

I'm so tired, you murmur.

I will be fine.

You shudder and close your eyes. You are struggling for each tedious, protracted breath now.

Let go.

You open your eyes. *I loved you so.*

I know.

Then you let go.

--Charlene Reddick

You Would Think That

after losing people you love you would think
that after years of it and the memorials
the ceremonies the dedications
and maybe the faces on the evening news
you'd think that might give a clue.
But so much hope or determination
written on their young lost faces.
So many of them.

You would think that eventually
it would become
somehow easier,
somehow you would be more wise
and certainly if the person who had
just died (we tend not to use that word
instead: lost, passed, gone)
was old, you would think
that grief would float more easily
down the river of your life,
in a different way.

But you see the photographs
of the young man in a B 2 bomber
or on the surfboard, smiling
as he flies in to shore
or the young woman on the motorcycle
behind her husband just as young
and it doesn't seem to be like that.

It seems we are always hit hard
a wreck, a side-swipe, out of the blue
even if we knew it was coming;
it wouldn't be long, soon or two weeks
or maybe six months.
Even if he's ninety

he still liked to walk on the beach
with his black lab
(who just died too)

and it's not really any different
than the first loss.
It's your own leaving
that hits you
after all.

--Judy Bebelaar

Symbiosis

Mushrooms pop up from
the mycelial web in the growing bed,
this ancient fungal relative that has survived
since the beginning of time
billions of years before us,
creating multiple pathways,
back-up plans to transport
resources, nutrients
and messages from plant to plant
across the garden, across thousands
of miles.

Decomposing dead leaves
and branches to create life,
new soil for plants to grow.

How we are hunched over
in our solitude and isolation
like a seed in the darkness
of the earth,

stretching arms out into
the great blue sky and sun
and wiggling our mycorrhizal toes
beneath us,
connecting with the whole.

                              --Teresa Mei Chuc

The Pedestrian, 2020

Louisa Winkler had had enough by the time they found her upstairs neighbor, Mr. Harvey, lying cold and dead on his creaky bedroom floor. Thirty days she had been locked away inside her apartment under what she called the draconian "stay-at-home" orders. She rarely ventured out unless it was to get the permissible groceries, booze, or medicine—thank *God* they let us eat and drink, she would say! But Sid Harvey hadn't left his place at all, for months, Louisa knew. He was *crippled*. There was no way he could have got the virus, she thought, let alone *died* from it! So, when she saw the warning notice taped to his door, complete with biohazard logo, stating that the place was contaminated with COVID-19, she lost it.

"Mom, that's *it*! I'm tired of this lockdown. I've had it –I'm *done*!" Louisa shouted to her mother, Emma, on the phone. "I'm going out! I'm going on a *walk*, in my own goddamn neighborhood. I need fresh air!"

"Louisa, *please*! Stop shouting. What are you talking about?"

"I'm talking about Sid Harvey, an invalid! He was *old*, and sick, and died of a heart attack or a stroke, and *they're* gonna say he died of the frickin' *coronavirus*!"

"Oh, don't start with *that*, Louisa…"

"*Sssh*!" Louisa said, pulling the phone away from her ear. "Do you hear that?"

She crept to her front door and looked through the peephole. She almost forgot that she had her mother on the phone. She caught a glimpse of several figures walking past her apartment door, dressed all in white biohazard suits, complete with masks, gloves, and boots. She thought she saw a gurney being dragged by one of them.

"Mom!" Louisa whispered loudly. "*They're* here! They've come for him."

"Who's come for him?"

"The guys in the *hazmat suits*! Those frickin'...biohazard—PPE—the all-white outfits with the gloves, and gas masks, and whatever else they bring with them!"

"They have to protect themselves, Louisa," Emma replied, an exasperated edge to her voice.

"That's what *they* tell you!" Louisa blurted, no longer afraid of who could hear her. "These guys in the white suits and masks, that show up in the nondescript white vans? Yeah, *they* come get you and take you away whether you have COVID or not. Whether you're *dead* or not! Just like in Wuhan! Dragging people out of their apartments, off the streets—never to be heard from again!"

"Oh, stop, Louisa! Just stop!" Emma retorted. "You and your crazy conspiracy theories—that's why you lost your job at the newspaper!"

"I was a threat!" Louisa retorted. "That's why I lost my job! For speaking the truth! And I'm not going to stand for this anymore! I'm going out! And I'm going out right now, without their dictator mask!"

She hung up on her mother. "Goddamn—*ugh*!" she said, grabbing her keys.

Louisa hadn't realized it was dark already as she stepped out into the still, warm air of the night. She looked up and down the street where she lived and was struck by how quiet it was. Aside from the cars parked along curb lines, there were little signs of life, not even sounds of dogs barking in the distance, or children crying from behind closed doors or curtained windows.

Louisa took a deep breath and smiled. She remembered that in months past, she would have been nervous walking down her street alone at night—a young, pretty woman, all by herself. There were some sketchy characters that used to stand around outside the stoop to their building, down near the corner. Sometimes they had beer kegs and she remembered crossing to the other side of the street, even in daylight, to avoid their catcalls.

But now the street's all mine, she thought, taking a deep breath and slowing her stroll on the uneven sidewalk.

She did not hear the car until it was alongside her. She saw it out of the corner of her eye and thought: *Where the hell did that car come from*? Was it *electric*, she wondered?

In an instant she was awash in a bright light coming from the car. She heard the crackle of a radio and heard the faint, metallic churning of the car's engine. She stopped and used her left hand, raised in front of her face, to block out the light. Cops? Louisa thought that maybe she should have brought her mask.

"Sorry," she thought to say. "I dropped my mask back there somewhere."

"What are you doing out here?" came a husky male voice.

If it *was* the police, they stayed inside their car, maybe trying to socially distance themselves.

"I'm just walking…"

"*Walking*?"

"Yeah, just taking a walk—I'm walking, down to the, uh…to the store—the *pharmacy*. I needed medicine."

"Where's your mask?" the officer asked.

Louisa squinted and leaned over, trying to get a better look at who was inside the car.

"I—I told you, I dropped it…back there."

"Why didn't you pick it up? That's littering."

Louisa sighed and lifted her hands up slightly, then let them drop back down to her sides.

"You're right, Officer," Louisa said. "I should have, uh, tried to pick it back up."

"Why aren't you sheltering in place at home?" asked a different officer, she could tell by the sound of his voice. She still couldn't see their faces due to the spotlight in her eyes.

"I needed medicine," she said, pointing down the street in the direction she was walking.

"There's no pharmacy in that direction," the first officer pointed out. "Where are you *really* going?"

"Y-yeah there is," she protested in as nice a way as possible. "At the Rite-Aid, down by, uh…"

"Down by Main and First," said the second officer. "That's in the *other* direction—behind you."

Louisa frowned and turned around. Then she looked back to where she had been headed, then just faced the police car.

"Yeah, I, uh…must have got turned around, officers. I think I'll just go home, call it a night, and try and order the medicine in the morning."

"Where do you live, Ms. Winkler?"

"Down by, uh…"

Louisa blinked several times, then leaned over again to get a look at the police.

"How did you know my name?" she asked.

"You *are* Louisa Winkler, the *journalist*?"

"Yeah, but…I don't work there anymore—how did you guys…?"

That's when she heard the sound of doors opening behind her. She turned in time to see five men in white biohazard suits walking toward her from a white van that had pulled into an adjacent driveway. They each had long, green rubber gloves and their faces were concealed behind black rubber breathing masks with reflective eye lenses. One of the men, the closest to Louisa, lifted a long, brass colored spray nozzle attached to a hose that wound down and around to a tank he carried on his back.

Louisa opened her mouth as if to scream just as he sprayed her face with something that smelled metallic but left an eerily sweet taste on her tongue. Her eyes widened in terror as her lips tingled and her throat started to swell. She couldn't scream because she couldn't breathe. They grabbed her arms and her legs and lifted her panicked form off the sidewalk. Before she lost consciousness, she saw that they were putting her into the back of the white van. Inside the cavernous dark, she had enough time to make out stacked forms wrapped in white sheets. They looked like people.

When the van doors closed and the men got back inside, the police car's spotlight switched off suddenly, and the squad car slowly drove off into the night.

--Victor Cass

---

*Inspired by Ray Bradbury's, "The Pedestrian," published August 7, 1951, in *The Reporter*, Los Angeles.

Serenity

serenity is
to be maskless
watching a woodpecker at the feeder
snipping the spent head of a petunia
lifting a magenta petal off a geranium leaf
a small healing I can accomplish

I have escaped the city
people who wear their masks around their necks
refuse to stay six feet apart
plant themselves mid-sidewalk on their phones
the FedEx woman whose boxes block the door
who says *I've got a job to do*
I have a daughter to feed
the guy in the park who says *You're an idiot*
when I say *Six feet please*
We both don't want to die

where the sand slips down toward the water
I park, my towels spread out like wings
to mark six feet on either side
a woman I see every day
her favorite spot the same as mine
tells her husband *Give her six feet*
He says *Even at the beach?*
as if the virus deserves a vacation

I can swim out far enough to be alone
serenity is
submerging myself in the ocean

-- **Elizabeth Zelvin**

After we choke and the virus leaves us, we return to the riversong

When I think of our river
I don't see boats
It's not a body of water either

More like blood
Like a swirl of intestines
Shoes without laces

Strings and beads of
Scapular and rosary

No water
Not our river
More like blood

Like a distant song
A lone guitar strum
A floating tombstone

The looming branches of the anacua
Take pity on this floating spine

Not a river
Not a river at all

More like a drool

--Edward Vidaurre

From A Newer World

I always searched for bottles on the shore. A message in a bottle! Nothing more and nothing less I'd take. I had the notion I'd receive a greeting from the ocean – not the slap of waves upon the sand, but some memento of a promised land. Not promised, really, that's too much to claim. But possible, at least. Today it came, my bottled message. Not what I had thought. No, it was much more than I'd ever sought. I had to read it twice. It was no hoax. Things like that are never merely jokes, on that I'd stake my life. I have. You'll see that when you read their notes, plus one from me.

> "So few are left who care for open spaces, fewer still for high and windy places unhedged with yielding things, who dream of mountains, not of meadows. People seem to care for plains, not peaks. They have no head for heights, so they prefer to live instead among the herd and never know their worth when ranged with giants (for here they walk the earth still), no. And sometimes I am sorry, for there are no others come to this world, nor, I fear, will any ever come. But let what will be, be. If any come, well met! So here's a hasty map. Though vague, it may suffice. Just follow the western stars. The way is there. I'll keep a double hope, not only for myself -- for comfort in those lonely nights when even stars are dark – for you, for any questing spirit, for the few souls who might share a hope without a name, and need the words to keep it bright. I claim my kinship with you, send to you my greeting and salute! Perhaps our only meeting, this. And yet I hope this bottled letter, conch-like, brings the echo of a better world. Remember the western stars. Their light is all you'll need for beacon in the night."

"Whoever, wherever you are, who's found this note, I haven't much to add to what he wrote. Or is it she? No matter, I suppose, except I'd love someone to love. God knows there isn't much in our gray world to miss...I'm off. To what was said, I'll just add this, that once one's soul has heard that far-off call from greater lands, from kindred souls, it's all one ever needs, that hope without a name. And I've no doubt that I shall find the same world he or she found, no doubt in the world. The map I shouldn't need. I'll leave it, curled up with the note, for you in case -- as I have, gone with no regrets -- you want to try the journey too. I won't be back. Please tell the others. Here's the map. Good luck. Fare well."

I've left the map, for where they are now, God alone knows. Pass the word. It might seem odd but, well, I'm off myself. The chances are, for good. Goodbye. Just follow the western stars, and take that nameless hope, and no regrets. We'll walk with giants before the last sun sets.

--Stephen Colley

We Will All Get Out of Here Alive

I have good news – we will all get out of here alive.
What happens, happens on time, don't seek your fault.
Nothing is your fault. There is no fault at all, but living,
through the mysteries of forgiving.
I see we are waiting for a miracle, the miracles happen
when I trust you, my sweetest friend, but nothing happens
when I cannot talk with you, and cannot keep my faith,
when I cannot continue my path when no one is around me,
when I cannot trust myself when all men doubt me.

Distance means nothing when your loved one means everything
and I am telling you – we will all get out of here alive.

What does not happen, does not happen in time, don't seek
your or others' fate. There is no fate at all, but choice,
in the centuries of noise and its deadly drive, while I am
telling you – we will all get out of here alive.

--**David Dephy**

Panoply of Gods

> *'Answer the highest calling of your heart and stand up for*
> *what you truly believe....the way of peace, the way of*
> *love and nonviolence is the more excellent way."*
> **--John Lewis**
> NY Times essay: July 30, 2020

I.

There is another panoply of gods that will not countenance
continuation
      of *meant-to-be*
         and *how-it's-been*
           and *shall-forever-be-amen,*
that will not blink as others did, souls blinkered, as numbers
numbed us weeks on end, numbed us to stolen generations of
wisdom, to holes gouged brutally in families, to savaging our
armies of healers.

Gods of gods and gods with gods, all gods since
you and I are gods,
will meld their spirits and birth a panoply unprophesied,
not parsed or plumbed, never seen, never prayed to or approached
with begging hands and bleeding knees,

gods unlike all that's gone before,
a panoply that spans diasporas of dessicated dreams, a pantheon
waiting in the wings for humankind to waken.

II.

We'll never return to the way things were, say all who calculate
caprices of change. *Things will never be the same again. No such thing
as getting 'back to normal.'*

The waiting panoply of gods nods, solemn in their work to come.

Post-pandemic roadmaps abound, with shamans, gurus, monks,
popes, seers, clerics, wizards, wiccans filling our breasts for eons
with wisdom pouring like healing honey from their core . . . .

poets, teachers, scholars, scribes, elders, deans, singers, weavers,
painters, sculptors building, honing, bending our cells to light . . . .

healers, medics, curanderos, farmers, pickers, drivers, transporters,
guardsmen, nannies, housekeepers, custodians, their weary bones
moving for us, giving, lifting, delivering, cleaning, proving that
'essential' comes from the dust and salt of earth
and holds no dollar signs.

III.

> *"They will say...*
> *that the heart, in those days,*
> *was small, and hard, and full of meanness."* [1]

John Lewis died in mid-July and America stood still,
reliving in bloody black/white reels beatings in Selma, Alabama,
cruel lawman clubs cudgeling John's skull,
unleashed dog fangs tearing peaceful skin of blacks
marching 60 years ago.

Hearts in those days were
> *small and hard,*
> *and full of meanness.*
But John's last words reverberated in marbled rotunda walls,
and around the world, words gilded in humanity and humility,
words pearlescent in transcendence, words clothed in blood
and sweat but filled with grace, words radiant with his goodness
and indomitable hope for a society of "love, brotherhood,
and true peace." [2]

IV.

Listen for a moment, my friends:
A better world awaits us when we heal again.
Like John Lewis, we can fight in peace and know that gods are not
the gods of old, for god is us, and we are wiser now.

Simplicity is often sacrificial to the other things --
things, mere things, golden rings, cadillacs, givenchy,
schooners, prada, tidal waves of soul-less things
that wormed their way into human *beings.*
Baubles that veneer us into thinking we've arrived and, like
a sorting machine, drop us into slots of grandiosity or poverty,
sifting, separating, clinking like coins in spirals of status,
endless pointed spirals boring into our hearts, impaling
humanity, drilling compassion away.

Simplicity is what John invoked, revered.
Simplicity has no dollar signs.

V.

> *"When this is over, the world must gather....*
> *The overriding goal must be human security."* [3]

The new panoply of gods flows its mantles of virtue and justice over
hamlets cleansed of poison, teeming crowds dissipated into
spaciousness, extended families toiling together, power meted out
to people (not plutocrats), children fed daily and taught with love.

This panoply of gods has no walls dividing nations, no skin hue
deemed superior, no woman menaced or defiled. No nuclear
weapons, arms race, or trillions in tanks. No dying oceans or reefs,
no arid farms, and no disease. Hands are clasped across oceans, not
clenched in catastrophic combat.

235

But first let's heal our nation, pave the way to
   new visions planted in democracy not demagoguery,
      in partnerships not paranoia,
         in egalitarianism not egotism,
            in humanitarianism not hubris.
John Lewis' final words to this world were:
   "Walk with the wind, brothers and sisters,
      and let the spirit of peace
         and the power of everlasting love
           be your guide."

The new panoply of gods awaits us in the wings
till we commit to these better things.

                     --Thelma T. Reyna

---

[1] Mary Oliver in her poem, "Of the Empire."
[2] John Lewis, his final essay, *New York Times,* July 30, 2020.
[3] Mikhail Gorbachev, "When This Is Over, the World Must Gather,"
   in TIME magazine, FINDING HOPE: SPECIAL REPORT,
   April 27-May 4, 2020.

This Annihilation

There is in this annihilation an opening
a wind whirling a ship out to sea

After the wedding the bride and groom return
home to tend the hearth and make bread

Somehow, the honey tastes sweeter
This dying and being reborn leaves me breathless

Drifting in a dreamless sleep, I feel the fire
on my beloved's lips

I am smoke drifting through an open door.

--Hazel Clayton Harrison

Afterword

by Mel Donalson, Ph.D.

In her 1937 novel, *Their Eyes Were Watching God*, Black author Zora Neale Hurston states: "There are years that ask questions and years that answer."[1] Currently, the United States is at a significant stage of weighing transformative questions that confront its citizens about the future structure and framework of the country.

When the Virus Came Calling: COVID-19 Strikes America offers poems, essays, and stories that explore those questions and their contemporary significance, capturing the powerful awareness of a devastating health issue while recognizing a corresponding awareness of the nation's political and moral health. This collection chronicles the first seven months of the year 2020, but the remaining months of the year are shadowed beneath gloomy clouds of confusion. When do we eradicate COVID-19, the historic novel coronavirus, and get back to normal? What happens to our national identity following the peaceful protests against violence rooted in racism? How will our society be different moving forward with or without this pandemic?

This book demonstrates the challenges of being *one* America, particularly when threatened by sources that seek to destroy the unified wholeness of the nation. In particular, several creative works assembled here reveal that viruses of "COVID-19" and "racism" are active concurrent agents of destruction. With intensified levels of anxiety and sobering data about staggering deaths due to this pandemic, Americans struggle daily with emotions that take them further from the stability usually offered by traditional holidays, entertainment, and sporting distractions, public activities, and personal events placed into our calendars of planning and expectations. Without those familiar signposts in their lives, with routines upended, people feel lost and adrift, as they float further out along an ocean of uncertainty and unanswered questions.

Looking backwards to forecast the future, we are reminded that America and the world have experienced other predatory diseases: the Spanish Flu (1918-1919); the Polio Epidemic (1950s); the Ebola Virus (1970s-present); the HIV-AIDS Virus (1980s-Present); the SARS Virus (2002); and the Swine Flu (2009). These epidemics were life-changing and overwhelming as they moved insidiously throughout the country and the world. With some diseases there were vaccines that eventually prevented or helped deliver a cure, but with other diseases, there were only medicines that ameliorated diseases and allowed people to live with them. Unfortunately, COVID-19 looms as one of those diseases that is predicted to be with our nation for some time to come, due in part to the chaotic, feckless response from our country's national leadership, their self-serving politicization of the virus, and the abundance of harmful partisan conspiracy theories, all leading to disunified, inconsistent crisis protocols and inaction, with states left to their own devices. As of this book's publication, the pandemic in America is in "free fall," as some scientists term it, and in most states of our country, it is not controlled. Perhaps because of all this, Americans will have to live with COVID-19 under the rubric of a "new normal" that enforces changes in daily patterns and behavior.

So how do we continue with life? In this time of living with dual viruses, the urgent need to recognize our interdependence for survival is stressed by numerous leaders globally, secular and non-secular. As South African activist Bishop Desmond Tutu emphasized in a speech about racial reconciliation, the African concept of "Ubuntu" was an essential element to transforming his country. He stated: "Ubuntu is the essence of being human. It speaks of compassion and generosity, of gentleness and hospitality and

240

sharing because it says my humanity is caught up in your humanity."[2] Coming together with compassion is vital to surmounting crises.

In an unexpected way, the prevalence of COVID-19 has divulged issues and ailments that have existed for generations within American society. COVID-19 has exposed the various systems within the U.S. that foster and maintain oppression of and discrimination against People of Color, the poor, disabled, LGBQT, immigrants, and other vulnerable, disenfranchised populations in our midst. The country's advancements in technology and communications have revealed the regressive and virulent practices and limitations that are firmly rooted in America's foundation of inequality. In particular, social media platforms and a free press have sharpened society's focus on racial biases and other far-flung inequities at the center of the country's legal and political arenas. Excessive partisanship and self-aggrandizement at the highest levels of the Executive, Congressional, and Judicial branches of government have all evoked anger and resistance within communities across racial and economic lines, amplified now during this COVID-19 pandemic.

In the early stages of the current civil unrest, as our nation daily, for over two months, marched in protest of racial injustice and police brutality, hope for America's future sprang from the alliances and commitments across racial, ethnic, generational, and economic backgrounds. Fault lines of America's entrenched inequalities in all arenas of life have been exposed, and the United States will *not* be the same anymore as our country moves forward. As the mounting statistics emphasize the death rates of citizens, small businesses, and public traditions around the country, America is being forced to face its vulnerabilities, not just to an enemy that challenges our best medical and scientific minds, but to our social structures as well. As Black author and political activist Cornel West asseverated in his book, *Race Matters*:

In these downbeat times, we need as much hope and courage as we do vision and analysis; we must accent the best of each other even as we point out the vicious effects of our racial divide and pernicious consequences of our maldistribution of wealth and power....We simply cannot enter the twenty-first century at each other's throats.[3]

Certainly, a treatment, or perhaps a cure, will eventually allow the country to adjust and live with COVID-19, but Americans must seize this place in time to do the hard-but-essential work of confronting, transforming, and hopefully eliminating the social inequality that infests the body of this country across all aspects of our lives. The American people must endure the painful, arduous work to unify and to rebuild the nation. The truths have been made self-evident by People of Color, history texts, news and information platforms, and, of course, the literary expressions found within this anthology.

We cannot merely regress to the way things have always been. A better future awaits us, all persons, regardless of race, class, gender, and religion.

❧

[1] Zora Neale Hurston. *Their Eyes Were Watching God*. Urbana: University of Illinois Press, 1980, p. 38.
[2] Kirsteen Kim, Editor. *Reconciling Mission: The Ministry of Healing and Reconciliation in the Church Worldwide*. ISPCK/UCA Publishers, 2005, p. 30.
[3] Cornel West. *Race Matters*. New York, Vintage Press, 1993, p. 159.

Appendix:
Cumulative Deaths in United States*
by Joshua Corwin

[First US infection: January 20, 2020]

Deaths	Dates
0	January 1
0	January 31
0	February 1
1 *[retroactive ID]*	February 29
0	March 1
3,170	March 31
60,966	April 30
103,781	May 31
126,140	June 30
154,320	July 31

৶

A Poetic Interpretation: The Color of Numbers

These numbers are colorless on the page, without race, religion, or creed; they have no hidden agenda. They are simply numbers. Exponential in their growth, they cause shadows to move and cast overhead tears from sky. I watch the hourglass, feel myself descend into quicksand. Will the last pebble on serenity's shore dwindle forever, succumb to nightfall, as numbers rise? Will our mosaic bodies be ethereal corpses and crash onto a nonexistent beach?

Will we further fragment—let our nation be riven, torn asunder by our own grenades of "do-nothing," "blame" and "noncompliance," and watch the aftermath of exploding numbers? Or will we unite as ocean—learn its secret truth? That ocean survives only if its moving parts stay together, while simultaneously accepting their reality, their confines, their shape?

---

* Data from European CDC. https://ourworldindata.org/covid-deaths

[EDITOR'S NOTE: My thanks to Joshua Corwin for assisting us with gathering data and for his poetic reflection upon it. His bio is below.]

Joshua Corwin, a Los Angeles native, is a neurodiverse, Pushcart Prize-nominated poet. His debut poetry collection, *Becoming Vulnerable* (2020), details his experience with autism, addiction, sobriety and spirituality. He has lectured at UCLA, and his Beat poetry is to be anthologized in late 2020, alongside Lawrence Ferlinghetti, Jack Hirschman, Michael C. Ford, Wanda Coleman, and Ruth Weiss. His collaborative book, *Ghosts Sing into the World's Ear*, with Ellyn Maybe, is scheduled for publication in September 2020. Corwin hosts the poetry podcast "Assiduous Dust" and holds a BA degree in mathematics. Visit his website at www.joshuacorwin.com

Authors' Gallery

Amy L. Alley

Khadija Anderson

RD Armstrong

Judy Bebelaar

Richard Blanco

Don Kingfisher
Campbell

Victor Cass

Teresa Mei Chuc

Carolyn Clark

Stephen Colley

David Dephy

Maija Rhee Devine

Seven Dhar

Linda Dove

Pauli Dutton

GT Foster

Martina Gallegos

Gerda Govine Ituarte

Tresha Faye Haefner

Peter J. Harris

Hazel Clayton Harrison

Michael Haussler

Marlene Hitt

Elline Lipkin

Radomir Vojtech
Luza

Alejandro Morales

Melinda Palacio

Judie Rae

Charlene Redick

Jimmy Recinos

Christine Reyna

Thelma T. Reyna

Lauren S. Reynolds

Mara Adamitz
Scrupe

Michael Sedano

Nancy Shiffrin

Cassie Premo Steele   Mary Langer   Maja Trochimczyk
                       Thompson

Edward Vidaurre   Angie Vorhies   Wanita Zumbrunnen

Elizabeth Zelvin   Robin D.G. Kelley   Mel Donalson,
                      INTRODUCTION   *AFTERWORD* & Poem

About the Authors

Amy L. Alley is an artist, writer, poet, educator who strives to bring her love of nature, line and flow to all her work. Her art is featured in public and private collections nationally and abroad. She recently worked in collaboration with Athens, GA.based Hippocampus Designs to design a skirt featuring her art. Her first novel, *The Absence of Anyone Else,* was published in 2010 and re- released as a second edition print with book club questions in Fall of 2018. She is the illustrator for poet Cassie Premo Steele's recent release, *The ReSisters.* Visit her blog about bold, creative living at www.boldnessinitiative.com. She lives in upstate South Carolina."

Khadija Anderson is the 2020-2022 Poet Laureate in Altadena, CA. Her poetry has appeared extensively in print and online. Her poetry book, *History of Butoh,* was published in 2012, and her chapbook, *Cul-de-sac: an american childhood* was released in June 2020. Khadija curates a monthly Social Justice themed poetry series in Pasadena, CA. She is a Muslim, mother, and Anarchist as well as a poet. Visit her online at khadijaanderson.com

RD Armstrong (aka **Raindog**) has 18 chapbooks and 9 books to his name and has been published in over 300 poetry magazines, anthologies and e-zines. He also operates the **Lummox Press** which has published over 100 issues of the **Lummox Journal;** and nearly 150 other titles including the chapbook series **Little Red Books** and the **Respect** perfect bound collections. The **Lummox Poetry Anthology** is one of his most important projects. Since 2012, he has been relying, in part, on poetry sales to survive on. Visit the website at www.lummoxpress.com/lc for ordering a book or two and help the guy out!

Judy Bebelaar's poems have been published in more than 50 literary journals and appear in several anthologies, including *The Widow's Handbook* (Foreword by Ruth Bader Ginsburg, *2014)* and the recent

California Fire & Water: a Climate Crisis Anthology, edited by Poet Laureate Molly Fisk (2020). Judy's chapbook, *Walking Across the Pacific,* was published by Finishing Line Press in 2014. Her nonfiction book, *And Then They Were Gone: Teenagers of Peoples Temple from High School to Jonestown,* co-authored with Ron Cabral in 2018, won 8 literary honors and awards. Judy taught in San Francisco's public high schools for 37 years. Her writing students won many awards, including 8 from at the national level, and Judy received national-level recognition for her teaching.

Richard Blanco was selected by President Barack Obama as the fifth inaugural poet in U.S. history. Blanco is the youngest and the first Latino, immigrant, and gay person to serve in such a role. Born in Madrid, Spain to Cuban exile parents and raised in Miami, FL, he is the author of memoirs and many collections of poetry, including his most recent, *How to Love a Country.* The negotiation of cultural identity characterizes his many collections of poetry, including *How to Love a Country,* which interrogates the American narrative and celebrates the still unkept promise of its ideals. He has also authored the memoirs *For All of Us, One Today: An Inaugural Poet's Journey* and *The Prince of Los Cocuyos: A Miami Childhood.* Blanco is currently an Associate Professor of Creative Writing at Florida International University.

Don Kingfisher Campbell, MFA, Antioch University, Los Angeles, taught at Occidental College Upward Bound for 35 years. He has been a coach and judge for Poetry Out Loud, a performing poet/teacher for Red Hen Press Youth Writing Workshops, LA Coordinator and Board Member of California Poets In The Schools, poetry editor of the *Angel City Review,* publisher of *Spectrum* literary magazine, organizer of the San Gabriel Valley Poetry Festival, and host of the Saturday Afternoon Poetry reading series in Pasadena, CA. For awards, features, and publication credits, please visit http://dkc1031.blogspot.com

Victor Cass is the author of four books: a history of the Pasadena (CA) Police Department; and three novels. His last novel, *Black Widow Bitches,* about an all-female, U.S. combat infantry unit in WWIII, won five national book awards. His fiction, poetry, and nonfiction have appeared in journals, anthologies, and print publications, including *If &When Literary Journal, Arroyo Monthly Magazine, Spectrum Anthology, Altadena Poetry Review Anthology, Mexican War Journal, Horror Sleaze Trash, Pasadena Weekly,* and the *Pasadena Star-News.* He received his BFA with Honors from Art Center College of Design, in Pasadena, CA, and his MA from American Military University in Manassas Park, VA. He was born in Kingsville, TX but was raised in his hometown of Pasadena, CA, where he is a 28-year-veteran of the police department.

Teresa Mei Chuc, Poet Laureate in Altadena, CA from 2018-2020, is the author of three full-length collections of poetry: *Red Thread* (2012), *Keeper of the Winds* (2014), and *Invisible Light* (2018). She was born in Saigon, Vietnam and immigrated to the U.S. under political asylum with her mother and brother shortly after the Vietnam War while her father remained in a Vietcong "reeducation" camp for nine years. Since the age of two, Teresa grew up in the Tongva village of Hahamongna, Pasadena, CA, where she still lives. Her poetry appears in journals such as *Consequence Magazine, EarthSpeak Magazine, Hawai'i Pacific Review, Kyoto Journal, Poet Lore, Rattle* and in anthologies such as *New Poets of the American West* (2010), *With Our Eyes Wide Open: Poems of the New American Century* (2014), *Inheriting the War: Poetry and Prose by Descendants of Vietnam Veterans and Refugees* (2017), and *California Fire & Water: A Climate Crisis Anthology* (2020). Teresa earned an MFA in Creative Writing at Goddard College in Plainfield, VT and teaches literature and writing at a public high school in Los Angeles.

Carolyn Clark, Ph.D., born in Ithaca, NY. often lived abroad. She studied Classics at Cornell, Brown and Johns Hopkins (diss. *Tibullus Illustrated: Lares, Genius and Sacred Landscapes*, 1998). Her recent poetry publications include *Poet Duet: A Mother and Daughter* (2019), *New Found Land* (2017), a pair of Finishing Line Press chapbooks – *Choose Lethe: Remember to Forget* (2017) and *Mnemosyne: the Long Traverse* (2013) – and winter poems in *The Avocet* (2017, 2018, 2019), all while moving back to the Finger Lakes region. Dr. Clark is a devoted teacher writing woodlands lyric poetry, and finding mythology everywhere.

Stephen Colley is a retired software engineer/manager who holds a B.S. in Physics from Pomona College and studied at the University of Redlands Graduate School of Music. He is the author of a poetry chapbook, *52 Poems* (a sort of Weekly Reader). He has also written three screenplays and classical music, including a song cycle on Lord of the Rings poems and settings of 13 Robert Frost poems. His poems have appeared in *Altadena Poetry Review* and in *California Quarterly*. He received an Honorable Mention in the *2019 Poets & Patrons* Helen Schible Contest; placed third in the 2019 *Writer's Digest* poetry contest; and was a 2019 Pushcart Prize in Poetry Nominee. He was also a Finalist in the 2018 *Oaxaca* Screenplay Competition and the 2019 *Socially Relevant* Screenplay Contest.

David Dephy is a trilingual Georgian/American award-winning poet, novelist, and multimedia artist. The winner of the 2019 Spillwords Press Poetry Award and the Finalist in the Adelaide Literary Award Anthology 2019 for the category of Best Poem. He is an active participant in the American and international poetry and artistic scenes, such as PEN World Voices, 92Y Poetry Center, Voices of Poetry, and Long Island Poetry Listings. The Bowery Poetry Club named him a Literature Luminary, and the *Statorec Magazine* named him an "Incomparable Poet." His works have been published and anthologized in USA and all over the world. Dephy is author of 15 books of poetry, 8 novels, and 3 audio albums of poetry. His first book-length works in English, a poetry *Lilac Shadow of a Tree* and *Eastern Star*, are forthcoming in USA in Spring/Fall 2020 from Mad Hat Press and Adelaide Books New York. His novel, *A Mystiere*, is forthcoming in USA in spring 2021 from Mad Hat Press. He lives and works in New York City.

Maija Rhee Devine's autobiographical novel about Korea, *The Voices of Heaven*, won four awards. Her prose and poems have appeared in *The Kenyon Review*, *North American Review*, her chapbook, *Long Walks on Short Days*, and anthologies. Her full-volume poetry manuscript, *Comfort Women: Freedom From Teeth*, was a Semi-Finalist in the 2019 *Crab Orchard Literary Journal* contest. The lead poem of the same title is scheduled for publication in *Pleiades*, June 2020. Her nonfiction and fiction works-in-progress deal with "comfort women" of WWII. She is a lecturer at the University of Washington, where she teaches various topics, including Comfort Women of World War II; and the Korean War. Her website is www.MaijaRheeDevine.com. She holds a Master's degree in English Literature from St. Louis University, Missouri.

Seven Dhar is Host of the Askew Reading Series Second Saturdays in Pasadena and the former co-host of the DTLA Poetry Meetup. He has been a Featured Performer at Mandy Kahn's Poetry Installation at the Philosophical Research Society 2020; and at LitFest Pasadena (with Poets in Distress) 2018. He was Rattle's Wrightwood Literary Festival and Poetry Slam Winner 2018; Winner of the SGV Poetry Festival chapbook contest for *Finnegan's Awake*; and the SGVPF broadside contest. His work has appeared in *Coiled Serpent, Lummox, We Didn't Cross the Border, the Border Crossed Us,* and Eagle Rock Library's anthology *The Stone Bird.* He is a graduate of UC Berkeley and UCLA.

Mel Donalson, Ph.D. is a multi-genre author and retired university professor. He taught at Bates College, UC-Santa Barbara, UCLA, California State University-Los Angeles, and Pasadena City College. His critical books include *Black Directors in Hollywood* (2003), *Masculinity in the Interracial Buddy Film* (2006), and *Hip Hop in American Cinema* (2007). He has also written three novels-- *The River Woman* (1988), *Communion* (2012), and *The Third Woman (Updated Edition,* 2018)--; various short films and plays, including *A Room Without Doors* (1998), *Performance* (2009), and *The Corner,* which was performed in the August 2017 Paul Robeson Theater Festival in Los Angeles; a full-length drama, *Shout* (2017), which was performed at the Fremont Theatre in South Pasadena, CA; and a full poetry collection, *Revelations* (2017). He has also edited two textbooks of African-American literature. He received his Ph.D. from Brown University. Contact Mel at www.meldonalson.com

Linda Dove holds a Ph.D. in Renaissance literature and teaches college writing. She is also an award-winning poet of four books: *In Defense of Objects* (2009), *O Dear Deer,* (2011), *This Too* (2017), and *Fearn* (2019), as well as the scholarly collection of essays, *Women, Writing,* *and the Reproduction of Culture in Tudor and Stuart Britain*. Her poems have been nominated for a Pushcart Prize, the Robert H. Winner Award from the Poetry Society of America, Best of the Net, and Best Microfiction. She lives in the foothills east of Los Angeles, where she serves as the faculty editor of *MORIA Literary Magazine* at Woodbury University.

Pauli Dutton received her MLS from University of Southern California. She founded, coordinated, and led the Altadena Library *Poetry and Cookies Anthology* and the companion annual public reading events from 2003-2014. She also wrote a poetry newsletter each year through 2013. She served on the Selection Committees for The *Altadena Literary Review* 2020 and the *Altadena Poetry Review* from 2015-2019. She co- edited the 2017 and 2018 editions. Dutton's poem, "Godparking," won Honorable Mention in *Shakespeare's Monkeys Review*, 2007. Her poem "To Be a Poet" tied for first place in the *Poetry.Blogspot* Thanksgiving Contest, 2009. Her work has also been published in the *Altadena Poetry Review*, the *Altadena Literary Review*, *Spectrum*, *San Gabriel Valley Poetry Quarterly*, *Poets on Site*, *Southern California Haiku Study Group Anthology*, the *Poetry and Cookies Anthology*, *Ribbons*, *Skylark*, *Mudpuppy*, the *Cherita Journal*, the *Pasadena Star News*, *The Stone Bird*, and *Imaginary Landscapes*. She is currently working on a book of poems about child abuse.

Gregory (GT) Foster, a 2017 Pushcart Prize Poetry Nominee, is a California native, retired educator, and Managing Editor of *Spectrum*, a poetry quarterly, and cohost of Saturday Afternoon Poetry in Pasadena, CA. He has published two poetry chapbooks and is in the home stretch of producing his first novel, *The Boys Are Not Refined*, a Vietnam-era semi-biographical soldier's story. His poetry has been published in *The Pasadena Weekly*, *San Gabriel Valley Quarterly*, *Spectrum*, *The Stone Bird Anthology 2016*, *Day of the Dead Anthology*, and *Altadena Poetry Review*.

Martina Gallegos is the author of numerous books, including *Grab the Bull by the Horns*, *Steppingstones*, *Home in a Bucket*, *Ode to Mother Nature*, and *From Poverty to University Graduate*. She came to California from Mexico before her fifteenth birthday and spoke no English.

She received her high school diploma and went on to earn a BA degree. She taught bilingually for 18 years until she suffered a work injury and subsequent near-fatal hemorrhagic stroke. She returned to school after her stroke and earned a Master's degree in 2015. Her work has appeared in Silver Birch Press, *Hometown Pasadena, SGVQR, Lummox, Spirit Fire Review,* and *Poetry SuperHighway.* She was named one of the Top Poets for the *Altadena Poetry Review: Anthology 2017,* and *San Gabriel Valley Quarterly.* A collection of her Spanish poetry will be released in late 2020.

Tresha Faye Haefner's work has been published in several journals, including *BloodLotus, The Cincinnati Review Fourth River, Hunger Mountain, Pirene's Fountain, Poet Lore, Prairie Schooner,* and *Rattle.* She is the recipient of the 2011 Robert and Adele Schiff Poetry Prize, the 2011 Alien Sloth Sex Award, a 2015 Pushcart Prize Poetry nominee, and author of two chapbooks, *The Lone Breakable Night* and *Take This Longing* from Finishing Line Press. Tresha is founder of The Poetry Salon, where she mentors writers. She has studied with poets such as Kim Addonizio, Sally Ashton, Jack Grapes, Suzanne Lummis, and founder of the Poetry Depths Mystery School, Kim Rosen. Find out more at www.ThePoetrySalon.com

Gerda Govine Ituarte, Ed.D. is the author of *Poetry Within Reach in Unexpected Places,* 2018; *Future Awakes in Mouth of NOW,* 2016; *Alterations | Thread Light Through Eye of Storm,* 2015; *Oh, Where is My Candle Hat?* 2012 (English and Spanish). She served as Editor of *Pasadena Rose Poets Poetry Collection 2019: Reflection. Resistance. Reckoning. Resurrection.* In the Summer of 2016, Govine Ituarte created a four-week reading series for the City of Pasadena Cultural Affairs Division and established the Pasadena Rose Poets. In February 2017, she created poetry readings at Pasadena City Council meetings that continue to this day. Her poetry has appeared in *Altadena Literary Review, Coiled Serpent, Journal of Modern Poetry, Ms. Aligned, Poets Salon* on ColoradoBlvd.net on Facebook and The Last Bookstore, and in the *Los Angeles Poet Society.* She was awarded an NEA grant and was a 2018 runner-up for the International Womyn's Month Poetry Contest. Website: www.poetryartbookstation.com

Peter J. Harris, a Writer & Cultural Worker, is the winner of many literary honors. He was a 2018 Los Angeles COLA Fellow in literary arts, Fellow of the Los Angeles Institute for the Humanities at USC. He is the author of *Bless the Ashes*, a poetry collection (Tia Chucha Press), winner of the 2015 PEN Oakland Josephine Miles Award; and *The Black Man of Happiness: In Pursuit of My 'Unalienable Right,'* personal essays, winner of a 2015 American Book Award. Harris has published his work in a wide variety of publications, including most recently: FICTION -- *Flint Hills Review* (2017), featuring a novel excerpt of "Magnificence," about an 'R&B Consultant and Vampire Whisperer'; *Onyx: International Journal* (2016); and *The Vampire Who Drinks Gospel Music: The Stories of Sacred Flow & Sacred Song* (2012); ESSAY -- *Los Angeles Review of Books* (2018); *Brooklyn & Boyle, Art & Life in Boyle Heights* (2012-2013); and POETRY-- LA Department of Cultural Affairs' *COLA Catalogue: ART* (2018); *Voices from Leimert Park Redux,* edited by Shonda Buchanan (2017); *Altadena Poetry Review: Anthology,* edited by Thelma T. Reyna, Poet Laureate of Altadena, CA (2014-2016); *Coiled Serpent: Poets Arising from the Cultural Quakes & Shifts in Los Angeles,* edited by Neelanjana Altadena Banerjee, Daniel A. Olivas, and Ruben J. Rodriguez (2016); and *Wide Awake: Poets of Los Angeles and Beyond,* edited by Suzanne Lummis (2015). He is founding director of The Black Man of Happiness Project, a creative, intellectual and artistic exploration of Black men and joy. Website: www.blackmanofhappiness.com/shop

Hazel Clayton Harrison served as Altadena Poet Laureate, Community Events, from 2018-2020. She worked closely with her co-Laureate, Editor-in-Chief, to edit the *Altadena Poetry Review 2019* and *Altadena Literary Review 2020*. Her recent book, *Down Freedom Road,* was published in 2020 by Shabda Press. Her poetry has been widely anthologized in literary journals, such as the *Altadena Literary Review 2020, Coiled Serpent, Grandfathers, A Rock Against the Wind,* and *River Crossings.* She is the author of a children's book, *The Story of Christmas Tree Lane.* Her memoir, *Crossing the River Ohio,* was released in 2014 and is available on Amazon. She is a co-owner and operator of Jah Light Media, a publishing and media consulting firm. As a member of the Pasadena Rose Poets ensemble, Hazel enjoys reading poetry with them at venues throughout Southern California.

Michael Haussler has been teaching in Los Angeles for 42 years. In 2002 he published his first book, a children's book, *Where is God's Prayer?* In 2011 he published his first novel about teaching high school, *Results May Vary.* Michael is a poet and loves writing and books. He is inspired by many things, but most of all by his wife, Teri. He believes that perhaps the best way to learn is to read; that reading frees us from space and time and allows us to go anywhere and do anything. He says, "If you love to learn, read. You will never be bored, and you will always make friends wherever you go."

Marlene Hitt was the first Poet Laureate in the successful Laureate series of Sunland-Tujunga (S/T) in Southern California. As an active member of the Village Poets of S/T, she participated in many readings and has been included in several anthologies, such as: *Chopin With Cherries* and *Meditations on Divine Names; Coiled Serpent,* an anthology of Los Angeles Poets edited by Luis Rodriquez; *Riddle in the Rain,* co-authored with Dorothy Skiles; and, most recently, a critically acclaimed poetry volume, *Clocks and Water Drops,* published in 2015. While serving in Bolton Hall Museum, Tujunga, she published more than 200 articles about local history in various newspapers. From these articles came her nonfiction book, *Sunland-Tujunga from Village to City,* published in 2000. Recent honors include Adam Schiff's "Woman of the Year" Award and recognition by State Legislator Anthony Portantino for service in the Sunland-Tujunga Neighborhood Council and in her community.

Robin D. G. Kelley, Ph.D. has served as Distinguished Professor and Gary B. Nash Endowed Chair in U.S. History at UCLA for several years. In his long academic career, he has taught at prestigious universities across America and abroad, including New York University, University of Michigan, University of Southern California, and Oxford. He is author of the acclaimed biography, *Thelonious Monk: The Life and Times of an American Original,* and other distinguished historical books, including *Freedom Dreams, Race Rebels,* and *Hammer and Hoe.* Dr. Kelley co-edited *Imagining Home.* He currently resides in Los Angeles.

Elline Lipkin, Ph.D. is a Research Scholar with UCLA's Center for the Study of Women and teaches poetry workshops in Los Angeles. She served as Poet Laureate in Altadena, CA from 2016-2018. As Laureate, she co-edited the *Altadena Poetry Review Anthology* in 2017 and in 2018, with Pauli Dutton, another Altadena poetry leader. Elline's poetry has been published in a range of contemporary journals, and she has been a resident at Yaddo, the Virginia Center for the Creative Arts, as well as the Dorland Mountain Arts Colony. She is the author of *The Errant Thread* and *Girls' Studies*.

Radomir Vojtech Luza was born in Vienna, Austria. He has been Poet Laureate of North Hollywood, CA since 2012. He was a Pushcart Prize Nominee (2012) and is the author of 30 books (26 collections of poetry). Luza's poetry has been published in over 60 literary journals, anthologies, websites, and other media, such as *Boston Globe, Los Angeles Daily News, Journal of Modern Poetry, Altadena Poetry Review*, and *2020 Altadena Literary Review*. Luza is also editor and publisher of the literary journal, *Voices in the Library*, published by Red Doubloon Publishing, and co-organizer/co-host of the poetry reading series, "UNBUCKLED: No Ho POETRY" at T.U. Studios in North Hollywood, CA. He graduated from Tulane University.

Alejandro Morales, Ph.D. the son of Mexican immigrants, was born in Montebello, CA, and grew up in Simons, the company town of the Simons Brick Yard #3, bordering Montebello. He earned his B.A. from California State University, Los Angeles; and an M.A. and Ph.D. from Rutgers University. Morales is currently a Professor Emeritus in the Department of Chicano/Latino Studies at the University of California, Irvine. He is the author of 11 books including, *The Captain of All these Men of Death* (2008); *River of Angels* (2014); and *Little Nation and Other Stories* (2014). A documentary film, "The Brick People," inspired by his novel *The Brick People*, was released in 2012. At present, he is working on several projects at different stages of development, including: *A Rainbow of Colors*, a biographical novel; a collection of speculative short stories; and *Zapote Tree*, his debut collection of poems scheduled to be published by Golden Foothills Press in Pasadena, CA in early 2021. Morales received the Luis Leal Award for Distinction in Chicano/Latino Literature in 2007 from the University of California, Santa Barbara.

Melinda Palacio is a poet, author, and speaker. She lives in Santa Barbara and New Orleans. Her poetry chapbook, *Folsom Lockdown*, won Kulupi Press' Sense of Place 2009 Award. Her novel, *Ocotillo Dreams* (ASU Bilingual Press, 2011) received the Mariposa Award for Best First Book at the 2012 International Latino Book Awards and a 2012 PEN Oakland-Josephine Miles Award for Excellence in Literature. Her first full-length poetry collection, *How Fire Is a Story, Waiting*, (Tia Chucha Press, 2012) was a finalist for the Milt Kessler Award, the Paterson Prize, and received First Prize in Poetry at the 2013 International Latino Book Awards. In 2015, her work was featured on the Academy of American Poets, Poem-a-Day Program. Melinda's latest poetry collection is *Bird Forgiveness*, 3. (Taos Press, 2018).

Judie Rae holds a Master's degree in Professional Writing. She is the author of four books for young people, including a Nancy Drew Mystery. She also authored a college thematic reader, *Rites of Passage* and two poetry chapbooks, *The Weight of Roses* and *Howling Down the Moon*, both published by Finishing Line Press. Her novel, *The Haunting of Walter Rabinowitz*, was published by Artemis Books in Fall, 2019. Her essays have appeared in *The Sacramento Bee*, as well as on San Francisco's NPR station KQED. She has also written for *Outside California, Tahoe Quarterly*, and *Sacramento Magazine*. After 27 years of teaching college English, Judie now concentrates on writing articles and essays primarily related to life in the Sierra Foothills.

Jimmy Recinos is a poet, writer, photographer, and podcaster in the city of Los Angeles. His blog, *JIMBO TIMES: The L.A. Storyteller*, has published literature, photography, and more from Los Angeles since 2014. When not writing, photo-walking, or organizing for youth and family education, Jimmy is recording for his new podcast, "J.T. The L.A. Storyteller Podcast," and getting his Los Cuentos merchandise-- an urban fashion brand dedicated to working-class Los Angelenos —in the public sphere, all for and all through Los Angeles, the place he calls home. He credits his mama, his first and foremost teacher, for all his work today.

Charlene Redick, Ph.D. is a Humana Festival playwright and a Williamstown Theatre Festival playwright. She is the recipient of awards for her fiction and poetry that include: the Dayton Playhouse; Fund for New Plays (Kennedy Center}; Coffeehouse Verse Competition (Huntington College; Writing Today Contest--Birmingham Southern College); The Playwright's Fund of North Carolina; Theatre Three Dallas; and The Southern Writers Project {Alabama Shakespeare Festival}. She is published by Samuel French, a contributor to the anthologies *Chinaberries and Crows*, and *Alabama Views and Words*. She was awarded the Kathryn Woodruff Fiction Writing Scholarship at the University of Tennessee-Knoxville. She is a Poetry Alum of the Sewanee Writers Conference and was nominated for the Susan Smith Blackburn Prize by the actor, Julie Harris. She can be reached at credick@mindspring.com

Christine Reyna, Ph.D. is currently a tenured Professor of Psychology at DePaul University in Chicago, and the founder of the Social and Intergroup Perceptions Lab. Her research focuses on stereotypes, prejudice, and intergroup relations with an emphasis on how people legitimize prejudice. She has examined these issues and their consequences on political and social policies including issues related to racism, affirmative action, LGBT policies, immigration, policing, and White nationalism. She has numerous academic publications on these topics in prestigious journals. Dr. Reyna served as the Associate Chair of her department for 6 years, where she developed a variety of policies and programs, including one of the nation's first pre-med specialization for psychology majors. She received her Ph.D. in Social Psychology from the University of California, Los Angeles.

Thelma T. Reyna, Ph.D. has won 16 national literary awards. She has written six books: a short story collection, *The Heavens Weep for Us and Other Stories;* two poetry chapbooks—*Breath & Bone* and *Hearts in Common;* and three full-length poetry collections—*Rising, Falling, All of Us; Reading Tea Leaves After Trump,* which won six national book honors in 2018; and *Dearest Papa: A Memoir in Poems,* (Golden Foothills Press, 2020). As Poet Laureate in Altadena, 2014- 2016, she edited the *Altadena Poetry Review Anthology* in 2015 . and 2016. Thelma's fiction, poetry, and nonfiction have appeared in literary journals, anthologies, textbooks, blogs, and regional media, print and online, for over 25 years. She was a Pushcart Prize Nominee in Poetry in 2017; and winner of a California state legislators' award, "Women in Business/ Author, Most Inspirational" in 2011. Thelma is the founder and owner of an editing consultancy, The Writing Pros, based in Pasadena, CA, and of the multiple-award-winning indie book publisher, Golden Foothills Press. She received her Ph.D. from UCLA. Visit her press' website at www.GoldenFoothillsPress.com

Lauren S. Reynolds is the author of two chapbooks and a full- length poetry collection. She has a Master's degree in Creative Writing, with a concentration in poetry and is a teacher of Art and English. Recurring themes in her writing include: memory, loss, coming of age and photography as an expression of the impermanence of time. These are narratives of a world that has moved on, and those who struggle to make ends meet. In addition to writing poetry, she enjoys reading, painting, and ballroom dancing with her husband, Nick. She lives in Dearborn, Michigan. She has taught high school Art, and currently, middle school English.

Mara Adamitz Scrupe, Ph.D. is a poet, visual artist and the author of six award-winning poetry collections, including *in the bare bones house of was; Eat the Marrow;* and *Beast.* Her poems have been published widely in national and international literary magazines and journals, including *London Magazine, Mid America Review, Maine Review, Rhino, Cincinnati Review,* and *Sentinel Quarterly Literary Review* (UK). Adamitz Scrupe has won or been shortlisted or nominated for many international poetry awards and prizes, including Canterbury International Arts Festival Poet of the Year (UK), Pushcart Poetry Prize (USA), Grindstone International Poetry Competition (UK), Fish Prize (Ireland), and Canberra Vice-Chancellor's Award (Australia). She is an art professor and Dean of the School of Art, University of the Arts, Philadelphia, USA.

261

Michael Sedano, Ph.D. writes the Tuesday column for *La Bloga*, the world's longest-continuously published Chicana Chicano Literature blog, of which he is a co-founder. He holds a Ph.D. in Communication Arts and Sciences from the University of Southern California, and is a veteran of the U.S. Army, 1969-70. He retired from the world of work after 24 years in private industry as a corporate offices factotum teaching Industrial Communications and Business Speech to sales, manufacturing, and warehouse employees in the U.S. and Canada. He is a staunch supporter of the literary arts, especially the work of Latina Latino authors in all genres and, in pre-pandemic times, hosted literary readings, "Living Room Floricanto," in his home in Pasadena, CA. He is also an experienced photographer whose photos are gallery-worthy.

Nancy Shiffrin, Ph.D. is the author of three poetry books: *The Vast Unknowing* (2012); *Game with Variations;* and *Flight*. She also published a novel, *Out of the Garden*, with accompanying essay, *Invoking Anaïs Nin*, from lulu.com. She has received awards and honorable mentions from The Academy of American Poets, The Poetry Society of America, The Alice Jackson Foundation, The Dora Teitelboim Foundation, and, most recently, first prize in the Angela Consolo Mankiewicz Poetry Contest, *Lummox Journal*, 2019. Her writing has appeared in the *Los Angeles Times, New York Quarterly, Earth's Daughters, Lummox Journal, The Canadian Jewish Outlook, A Cafe in Space, Religion and Literature, Shofar*, and numerous other publications. Nancy earned her MA degree in English studying with Anaïs Nin. She earned her Ph.D. at The Union Institute studying Jewish-American women authors.

Cassie Premo Steele, Ph.D. is an ecofeminist poet, novelist, and the author of 16 books, including six books of poetry. Her poetry has been nominated six times for the Pushcart Prize. She is a recipient of The Archibald Rutledge Prize and The John Edward Johnson Prize, both sponsored by the Poetry Society of South Carolina. She won the First Place Award in the Recycled Words Nature Poetry Competition, as well as an Annual Literary Award from the Sumter County Cultural Commission. She received several Honorable Mentions and was a Top Ten Finalist in *The State* newspaper and University of South Carolina's Poetry Initiative's Annual Poetry Contest. She received the Carrie McCray Literary Award for Poetry sponsored by the South Carolina Writers Workshop, and she was a Finalist for the Rita Dove Poetry Award judged by Joy Harjo. She lives with her wife and college-aged daughter in Columbia, South Carolina. Her website is www.cassiepremosteele.com

Mary Langer Thompson, Ed.D. was the 2012 Senior Poet Laureate of California. Her poems, short stories, and essays appear in various journals and anthologies. She is a contributor to two poetry writing texts, *The Working Poet* (Autumn Press, 2009) and *Women and Poetry: Writing, Revising, Publishing and Teaching* (McFarland, 2012). Her children's books-- *How the Blue-Tongued Skink got his Blue Tongue* and *The Gull Who Thought He Was Dull*-- were published by Another Think Coming Press. A retired school principal and former secondary English teacher, Langer Thompson received her Ed.D. from the University of California, Los Angeles. She continues to enjoy conducting writing workshops for schools, prisons, and in her community where she won the 2019 Jack London Award from the California Writers Club, High Desert Branch.

Maja Trochimczyk, Ph.D. is a Polish-born California poet, music historian, and photographer. She has published seven books on music and five collections of poetry (*Rose Always, Miriam's Iris, Slicing the Bread, Into Light,* and *The Rainy Bread*). She edited four poetry anthologies; *Chopin with Cherries, Meditations on Divine Names, Grateful Conversations,* and *We Are Here: Village Poets Anthology.* She also wrote hundreds of book chapters, peer-reviewed articles and poems published in English, Polish and many translations. She is the founder of Moonrise Press and a member of poetry groups Westside Women Writers and Village Poets. She also serves as the President of the California State Poetry Society, the President of Helena Modjeska Art and Culture Club, and the Senior Director of Planning and Development for Phoenix House California. Visit her website at www.moonrisepress.com

Edward Vidaurre is the author of 6 collections of poetry. He is the 2018-2019 City of McAllen, TX Poet Laureate; a four-time Pushcart Prize Nominee for poetry; and publisher of FlowerSong Press and its sister imprint, Juventud Press. His writings have appeared or are forthcoming in the following: *The New York Times Magazine, The Texas Observer, Grist, Poet Lore, The Acentos Review, Poetrybay, Voices de la Luna,* as well as other journals and anthologies. Vidaurre has been a judge for submissions for the Houston Poetry Festival; editor for the Rio Grande Valley International Poetry Festival anthology *Boundless 2020;* and editor of *Cutthroat,* a journal of the arts. Vidaurre is from Boyle Heights, CA and now resides in McAllen, TX with his wife and daughter.

Angie Vorhies is a poet, documentarian, and co-founder of San Diego Roots, a non-profit dedicated to educating, empowering, and cultivating sustainable local food communities. Her writing has appeared in *Poetry International, Orion Magazine, Atlanta Review,* and *Notre Dame Review.* She recently received her certificate in documentary filmmaking from the Center for Documentary Studies at Duke University and makes poem-films focusing on social and environmental justice.

Wanita Zumbrunnen is an Adjunct Professor at Lindenwood University in St. Charles, MO. She has won awards at the St. Louis Poetry Center, and has appeared in *Inspirations, The Cloverdale Review, Slate, Daily Palette,* and received International Publication Awards in 1996 and 2000 from the *Atlanta Review.* In 2012, Finishing Line Press published her chapbook, *All Mortals Shall Dream Dreams.* In June 2014, she was invited to a Writers Conference in Como, Italy, where workshops were led by Pulitzer Prize winner, Rae Armantrout, and National Poetry prize winner, Nikki Finney. Wanita taught English and speech on military bases in Japan, Germany, Turkey, and Kosovo; and received two Fulbright Scholarships for her teaching in Pakistan. Wanita lives in St. Louis, MO.

Elizabeth Zelvin, from New York City, is the author of the Bruce Kohler Mysteries and the Jewish historical Mendoza Family Saga. She is also editor of two anthologies, *Me Too Short Stories* (crimes against women, tales of retribution and healing) and *Where Crime Never Sleeps*. Liz's stories have been nominated three times each for the Agatha and Derringer Awards for Best Short Story. Another story was listed in *Best American Mysteries 2014*. Liz is also a New York psychotherapist who works with clients all over the world as an online therapist. In addition, as Liz Zelvin, she is a singer-songwriter whose album of original songs is titled "Outrageous Older Woman." Her author website is at www.elizabethzelvin.com

SPACE FOR NOTES